Dear reader,

thank you for your trust and for buying this book. I'm always greatly moved when I see someone with a desire to get closer to God, to accept Him as their Lord and Saviour and invite Him into their everyday life, to each and every part of it.

By studying His Word systematically, each and every day is a day we live with Him, we let Him illuminate the path of our lives.

I am glad that together we can walk this wonderful path. I ask each of you to pray for me, and I, for my part, promise to remember each and every one of you in my prayers.

Before every encounter with the Lord in His Word, let us pray to the Holy Spirit, may He guide us, for He is the true author of this Word and, at the same time, He knows us better than anyone else, better even than we know ourselves. May He speak directly to our hearts, our minds. May He enter with His Word into our lives, into all our affairs - the pleasant ones as well as the difficult ones

After praying to the Holy Spirit, let us read a given passage of the Scripture. Let's do this slowly, we may even repeat it several times. The Lord will speak to us sometimes through a whole passage, sometimes through a single sentence or word. Sometimes He speaks immediately, sometimes He speaks subtly, after a long time.

Let's write down what the Lord wants to say through the given passage. His Word will sustain us as we remember it throughout the day, act and live with it, with HIM.

May The Lord in Heaven bless you, dear reader. Amen.

CONTENTS

PRINCIPAL CELEBRATIONS OF THE LITURGICAL YEAR 2025

First Sunday of Advent	December 1, 2024
Ash Wednesday	March 5, 2025
Easter Sunday	April 20, 2025
The Ascension of the Lord [Thursday]	May 29, 2025
Pentecost Sunday	June 8, 2025
The Most Holy Body and Blood of Christ	June 22, 2025
First Sunday of Advent	November 30, 2025

CYCLES — LECTIONARY FOR MASS

Sunday Cycle	YEAR C	December 1, 2024 to November 23, 2025
Weekday Cycle	CYCLE I	January 13 to March 4, 2025 June 9 to November 29, 2025
Sunday Cycle	YEAR A	November 30, 2025 to November 22, 2026

Wednesday, January 1, 2025
SOLEMNITY OF MARY, THE HOLY MOTHER OF GOD

First Reading: Numbers 6: 22-27

22 Yahweh spoke to Moses, saying, 23 "Speak to Aaron and to his sons, saying, 'This is how you shall bless the children of Israel.' You shall tell them, 24 'Yahweh bless you, and keep you. 25 Yahweh make his face to shine on you, and be gracious to you. 26 Yahweh lift up his face toward you, and give you peace.' 27 "So they shall put my name on the children of Israel; and I will bless them."

Responsorial Psalm: Psalms 67: 2-3, 5, 6, 8

2 That your way may be known on earth,
and your salvation among all nations,
3 let the peoples praise you, God.
Let all the peoples praise you.
5 Let the peoples praise you, God.
Let all the peoples praise you.
6 The earth has yielded its increase.
God, even our own God, will bless us.
8 God will bless us.
All the ends of the earth shall fear him.

Second Reading: Galatians 4: 4-7

4 But when the fullness of the time came, God sent out his Son, born to a woman, born under the law, 5 that he might redeem those who were under the law, that we might receive the adoption as children. 6 And because you are children, God sent out the Spirit of his Son into your hearts, crying, "Abba,† Father!" 7 So you are no longer a bondservant, but a son; and if a son, then an heir of God through Christ.

Gospel: Luke 2: 16-21

16 They came with haste and found both Mary and Joseph, and the baby was lying in the feeding trough. 17 When they saw it, they publicized widely the saying which was spoken to them about this child. 18 All who heard it wondered at the things which were spoken to them by the shepherds. 19 But Mary kept all these sayings, pondering them in her heart. 20 The shepherds returned, glorifying and praising God for all the things that they had heard and seen, just as it was told them. 21 When eight days were fulfilled for the

circumcision of the child, his name was called Jesus, which was given by the angel before he was conceived in the womb.

1. Invite the Holy Spirit into this reading, asking the Author of Scripture to speak to you through His Word
2. Read today's passage as many times as you need, take your time
3. Write down (below) what the Lord is saying to you today
4. Live with this Word in your heart through the day

_____

_____

Sunday, January 5, 2025
THE EPIPHANY OF THE LORD

First Reading: Isaiah 60: 1-6

[1] "Arise, shine; for your light has come,
and Yahweh's glory has risen on you!
[2] For behold, darkness will cover the earth,
and thick darkness the peoples;
but Yahweh will arise on you,
and his glory shall be seen on you.
[3] Nations will come to your light,
and kings to the brightness of your rising.

[4] "Lift up your eyes all around, and see:
they all gather themselves together.
They come to you.
Your sons will come from far away,
and your daughters will be carried in arms.
[5] Then you shall see and be radiant,
and your heart will thrill and be enlarged;
because the abundance of the sea will be turned to you.
The wealth of the nations will come to you.
[6] A multitude of camels will cover you,
the dromedaries of Midian and Ephah.
All from Sheba will come.

They will bring gold and frankincense,
and will proclaim the praises of Yahweh.

Responsorial Psalm: Psalms 72: 1-2, 7-8, 10-13

[1] God, give the king your justice;
your righteousness to the royal son.
[2] He will judge your people with righteousness,
and your poor with justice.
[7] In his days, the righteous shall flourish,
and abundance of peace, until the moon is no more.
[8] He shall have dominion also from sea to sea,
from the River to the ends of the earth.
[10] The kings of Tarshish and of the islands will bring tribute.
The kings of Sheba and Seba shall offer gifts.
[11] Yes, all kings shall fall down before him.
All nations shall serve him.
[12] For he will deliver the needy when he cries;
the poor, who has no helper.
[13] He will have pity on the poor and needy.
He will save the souls of the needy.

Second Reading: Ephesians 3: 2-3a, 5-6

2 if it is so that you have heard of the administration of that grace of God which was given me toward you, 3 how that by revelation the mystery was made known to me, 5 which in other generations was not made known to the children of men, as it has now been revealed to his holy apostles and prophets in the Spirit, 6 that the Gentiles are fellow heirs and fellow members of the body, and fellow partakers of his promise in Christ Jesus through the Good News

Gospel: Matthew 2: 1-12

1 Now when Jesus was born in Bethlehem of Judea in the days of King Herod, behold, wise men† from the east came to Jerusalem, saying, 2 "Where is he who is born King of the Jews? For we saw his star in the east, and have come to worship him." 3 When King Herod heard it, he was troubled, and all Jerusalem with him. 4 Gathering together all the chief priests and scribes of the people, he asked them where the Christ would be born. 5 They said to him, "In Bethlehem of Judea, for this is written through the prophet,
6 'You Bethlehem, land of Judah,

are in no way least among the princes of Judah;
for out of you shall come a governor
who shall shepherd my people, Israel.' "*
7 Then Herod secretly called the wise men, and learned from them exactly what time the star appeared. 8 He sent them to Bethlehem, and said, "Go and search diligently for the young child. When you have found him, bring me word, so that I also may come and worship him."
9 They, having heard the king, went their way; and behold, the star, which they saw in the east, went before them until it came and stood over where the young child was. 10 When they saw the star, they rejoiced with exceedingly great joy. 11 They came into the house and saw the young child with Mary, his mother, and they fell down and worshiped him. Opening their treasures, they offered to him gifts: gold, frankincense, and myrrh. 12 Being warned in a dream not to return to Herod, they went back to their own country another way.

1. Invite the Holy Spirit into this reading, asking the Author of Scripture to speak to you through His Word
2. Read today's passage as many times as you need, take your time
3. Write down (below) what the Lord is saying to you today
4. Live with this Word in your heart through the day

_____

_____

Sunday, January 12, 2025
THE BAPTISM OF THE LORD

First Reading: Isaiah 42: 1-4, 6-7

[1] "Behold, my servant, whom I uphold,
my chosen, in whom my soul delights:
I have put my Spirit on him.
He will bring justice to the nations.
[2] He will not shout,
nor raise his voice,
nor cause it to be heard in the street.
[3] He won't break a bruised reed.
He won't quench a dimly burning wick.

He will faithfully bring justice.
4 He will not fail nor be discouraged,
until he has set justice in the earth,
and the islands wait for his law."
6 "I, Yahweh, have called you in righteousness.
I will hold your hand.
I will keep you,
and make you a covenant for the people,
as a light for the nations,
7 to open the blind eyes,
to bring the prisoners out of the dungeon,
and those who sit in darkness out of the prison.

Responsorial Psalm: Psalms 104: 1b-4, 24-25, 27-30

1b Yahweh, my God, you are very great.
You are clothed with honor and majesty.
2 He covers himself with light as with a garment.
He stretches out the heavens like a curtain.
3 He lays the beams of his rooms in the waters.
He makes the clouds his chariot.
He walks on the wings of the wind.
4 He makes his messengers⊥ winds,
and his servants flames of fire.
24 Yahweh, how many are your works!
In wisdom, you have made them all.
The earth is full of your riches.
25 There is the sea, great and wide,
in which are innumerable living things,
both small and large animals.
27 These all wait for you,
that you may give them their food in due season.
28 You give to them; they gather.
You open your hand; they are satisfied with good.
29 You hide your face; they are troubled.
You take away their breath; they die and return to the dust.
30 You send out your Spirit and they are created.
You renew the face of the ground.

Second Reading: Titus 2: 11-14; 3: 4-7

[11] For the grace of God has appeared, bringing salvation to all men, [12] instructing us to the intent that, denying ungodliness and worldly lusts, we would live soberly, righteously, and godly in this present age; [13] looking for the blessed hope and appearing of the glory of our great God and Savior, Jesus Christ, [14] who gave himself for us, that he might redeem us from all iniquity and purify for himself a people for his own possession, zealous for good works.

[4] But when the kindness of God our Savior and his love toward mankind appeared, [5] not by works of righteousness which we did ourselves, but according to his mercy, he saved us through the washing of regeneration and renewing by the Holy Spirit, [6] whom he poured out on us richly through Jesus Christ our Savior; [7] that being justified by his grace, we might be made heirs according to the hope of eternal life.

Gospel: Luke 3: 15-16, 21-22

[15] As the people were in expectation, and all men reasoned in their hearts concerning John, whether perhaps he was the Christ, [16] John answered them all, "I indeed baptize you with water, but he comes who is mightier than I, the strap of whose sandals I am not worthy to loosen. He will baptize you in the Holy Spirit and fire.

[21] Now when all the people were baptized, Jesus also had been baptized and was praying. The sky was opened, [22] and the Holy Spirit descended in a bodily form like a dove on him; and a voice came out of the sky, saying "You are my beloved Son. In you I am well pleased."

1. Invite the Holy Spirit into this reading, asking the Author of Scripture to speak to you through His Word
2. Read today's passage as many times as you need, take your time
3. Write down (below) what the Lord is saying to you today
4. Live with this Word in your heart through the day

_____

_____

Sunday, January 19, 2025
SECOND SUNDAY IN ORDINARY TIME

First Reading: Isaiah 62: 1-5

[1] For Zion's sake I will not hold my peace,

and for Jerusalem's sake I will not rest,
until her righteousness shines out like the dawn,
and her salvation like a burning lamp.
2 The nations will see your righteousness,
and all kings your glory.
You will be called by a new name,
which Yahweh's mouth will name.
3 You will also be a crown of beauty in Yahweh's hand,
and a royal diadem in your God's hand.
4 You will not be called Forsaken any more,
nor will your land be called Desolate any more;
but you will be called Hephzibah,†
and your land Beulah;‡
for Yahweh delights in you,
and your land will be married.
5 For as a young man marries a virgin,
so your sons will marry you.
As a bridegroom rejoices over his bride,
so your God will rejoice over you.

Responsorial Psalm: Psalms 96: 1-3, 7-10

1 Sing to Yahweh a new song!
Sing to Yahweh, all the earth.
2 Sing to Yahweh!
Bless his name!
Proclaim his salvation from day to day!
3 Declare his glory among the nations,
his marvelous works among all the peoples.
7 Ascribe to Yahweh, you families of nations,
ascribe to Yahweh glory and strength.
8 Ascribe to Yahweh the glory due to his name.
Bring an offering, and come into his courts.
9 Worship Yahweh in holy array.
Tremble before him, all the earth.
10 Say among the nations, "Yahweh reigns."
The world is also established.
It can't be moved.
He will judge the peoples with equity.

Second Reading: First Corinthians 12: 4-11

4 Now there are various kinds of gifts, but the same Spirit. 5 There are various kinds of service, and the same Lord. 6 There are various kinds of workings, but the same God who works all things in all. 7 But to each one is given the manifestation of the Spirit for the profit of all. 8 For to one is given through the Spirit the word of wisdom, and to another the word of knowledge according to the same Spirit, 9 to another faith by the same Spirit, and to another gifts of healings by the same Spirit, 10 and to another workings of miracles, and to another prophecy, and to another discerning of spirits, to another different kinds of languages, and to another the interpretation of languages. 11 But the one and the same Spirit produces all of these, distributing to each one separately as he desires.

Gospel: John 2: 1-11

1 The third day, there was a wedding in Cana of Galilee. Jesus' mother was there. 2 Jesus also was invited, with his disciples, to the wedding. 3 When the wine ran out, Jesus' mother said to him, "They have no wine."
4 Jesus said to her, "Woman, what does that have to do with you and me? My hour has not yet come."
5 His mother said to the servants, "Whatever he says to you, do it."
6 Now there were six water pots of stone set there after the Jews' way of purifying, containing two or three metretes± apiece. 7 Jesus said to them, "Fill the water pots with water." So they filled them up to the brim. 8 He said to them, "Now draw some out, and take it to the ruler of the feast." So they took it. 9 When the ruler of the feast tasted the water now become wine, and didn't know where it came from (but the servants who had drawn the water knew), the ruler of the feast called the bridegroom 10 and said to him, "Everyone serves the good wine first, and when the guests have drunk freely, then that which is worse. You have kept the good wine until now!" 11 This beginning of his signs Jesus did in Cana of Galilee, and revealed his glory; and his disciples believed in him.

1. Invite the Holy Spirit into this reading, asking the Author of Scripture to speak to you through His Word
2. Read today's passage as many times as you need, take your time
3. Write down (below) what the Lord is saying to you today
4. Live with this Word in your heart through the day

Sunday, January 26, 2025
THIRD SUNDAY IN ORDINARY TIME

First Reading: Nehemiah 8: 2-4a, 5-6, 8-10

2 Ezra the priest brought the law before the assembly, both men and women, and all who could hear with understanding, on the first day of the seventh month. 3 He read from it before the wide place that was in front of the water gate from early morning until midday, in the presence of the men and the women, and of those who could understand. The ears of all the people were attentive to the book of the law. 4a Ezra the scribe stood on a pulpit of wood, which they had made for the purpose; 5 Ezra opened the book in the sight of all the people (for he was above all the people), and when he opened it, all the people stood up. 6 Then Ezra blessed Yahweh, the great God.

All the people answered, "Amen, Amen," with the lifting up of their hands. They bowed their heads, and worshiped Yahweh with their faces to the ground.

8 They read in the book, in the law of God, distinctly; and they gave the sense, so that they understood the reading.

9 Nehemiah, who was the governor, Ezra the priest and scribe, and the Levites who taught the people said to all the people, "Today is holy to Yahweh your God. Don't mourn, nor weep." For all the people wept when they heard the words of the law. 10 Then he said to them, "Go your way. Eat the fat, drink the sweet, and send portions to him for whom nothing is prepared, for today is holy to our Lord. Don't be grieved, for the joy of Yahweh is your strength."

Responsorial Psalm: Psalms 19: 8, 9, 10, 15

8 Yahweh's precepts are right, rejoicing the heart.
Yahweh's commandment is pure, enlightening the eyes.
9 The fear of Yahweh is clean, enduring forever.
Yahweh's ordinances are true, and righteous altogether.
10 They are more to be desired than gold, yes, than much fine gold,
sweeter also than honey and the extract of the honeycomb.
15 Let the words of my mouth and the meditation of my heart
be acceptable in your sight,
Yahweh, my rock, and my redeemer.

Second Reading: First Corinthians 12: 12-14, 27

[12] For as the body is one and has many members, and all the members of the body, being many, are one body; so also is Christ. [13] For in one Spirit we were all baptized into one body, whether Jews or Greeks, whether bond or free; and were all given to drink into one Spirit. [14] For the body is not one member, but many.

[27] Now you are the body of Christ, and members individually.

Gospel: Luke 1: 1-4; 4: 14-21

[1] Since many have undertaken to set in order a narrative concerning those matters which have been fulfilled among us, [2] even as those who from the beginning were eyewitnesses and servants of the word delivered them to us, [3] it seemed good to me also, having traced the course of all things accurately from the first, to write to you in order, most excellent Theophilus; [4] that you might know the certainty concerning the things in which you were instructed.

[14] Jesus returned in the power of the Spirit into Galilee, and news about him spread through all the surrounding area. [15] He taught in their synagogues, being glorified by all.

[16] He came to Nazareth, where he had been brought up. He entered, as was his custom, into the synagogue on the Sabbath day, and stood up to read. [17] The book of the prophet Isaiah was handed to him. He opened the book, and found the place where it was written,

[18] "The Spirit of the Lord is on me,

because he has anointed me to preach good news to the poor.

He has sent me to heal the broken hearted,[‡]

to proclaim release to the captives,

recovering of sight to the blind,

to deliver those who are crushed,

[19] and to proclaim the acceptable year of the Lord."[*]

[20] He closed the book, gave it back to the attendant, and sat down. The eyes of all in the synagogue were fastened on him. [21] He began to tell them, "Today, this Scripture has been fulfilled in your hearing."

1. Invite the Holy Spirit into this reading, asking the Author of Scripture to speak to you through His Word
2. Read today's passage as many times as you need, take your time
3. Write down (below) what the Lord is saying to you today
4. Live with this Word in your heart through the day

_____

_____

Sunday, February 2, 2025
THE PRESENTATION OF THE LORD

First Reading: Malachi 3: 1-4

[1] "Behold, I send my messenger, and he will prepare the way before me! The Lord, whom you seek, will suddenly come to his temple. Behold, the messenger of the covenant, whom you desire, is coming!" says Yahweh of Armies. [2] "But who can endure the day of his coming? And who will stand when he appears? For he is like a refiner's fire, and like launderers' soap; [3] and he will sit as a refiner and purifier of silver, and he will purify the sons of Levi, and refine them as gold and silver; and they shall offer to Yahweh offerings in righteousness. [4] Then the offering of Judah and Jerusalem will be pleasant to Yahweh as in the days of old and as in ancient years.

Responsorial Psalm: Psalms 24: 7-10

[7] Lift up your heads, you gates!
Be lifted up, you everlasting doors,
and the King of glory will come in.
[8] Who is the King of glory?
Yahweh strong and mighty,
Yahweh mighty in battle.
[9] Lift up your heads, you gates;
yes, lift them up, you everlasting doors,
and the King of glory will come in.
[10] Who is this King of glory?
Yahweh of Armies is the King of glory!

Second Reading: Hebrews 2: 14-18

[14] Since then the children have shared in flesh and blood, he also himself in the same way partook of the same, that through death he might bring to nothing him who had the power of death, that is, the devil, [15] and might deliver all of them who through fear of death were all their lifetime subject to bondage. [16] For most certainly, he doesn't give help to angels, but he gives help to the offspring[§] of Abraham. [17] Therefore he was obligated in all things to be made like his brothers, that he might become a merciful and faithful high priest in things pertaining to God, to make atonement for the sins of the people. [18] For in that he himself has suffered being tempted, he is able to help those who are tempted.

Gospel: Luke 2: 22-32

22 When the days of their purification according to the law of Moses were fulfilled, they brought him up to Jerusalem to present him to the Lord 23 (as it is written in the law of the Lord, "Every male who opens the womb shall be called holy to the Lord"),* 24 and to offer a sacrifice according to that which is said in the law of the Lord, "A pair of turtledoves, or two young pigeons."*

25 Behold, there was a man in Jerusalem whose name was Simeon. This man was righteous and devout, looking for the consolation of Israel, and the Holy Spirit was on him. 26 It had been revealed to him by the Holy Spirit that he should not see death before he had seen the Lord's Christ.‡ 27 He came in the Spirit into the temple. When the parents brought in the child, Jesus, that they might do concerning him according to the custom of the law, 28 then he received him into his arms and blessed God, and said,

29 "Now you are releasing your servant, Master,
according to your word, in peace;
30 for my eyes have seen your salvation,
31 which you have prepared before the face of all peoples;
32 a light for revelation to the nations,
and the glory of your people Israel."

1. Invite the Holy Spirit into this reading, asking the Author of Scripture to speak to you through His Word
2. Read today's passage as many times as you need, take your time
3. Write down (below) what the Lord is saying to you today
4. Live with this Word in your heart through the day

_____

_____

Sunday, February 9, 2025
FIFTH SUNDAY IN ORDINARY TIME

First Reading: Isaiah 6: 1-2a, 3-8

1 In the year that King Uzziah died, I saw the Lord sitting on a throne, high and lifted up; and his train filled the temple. 2a Above him stood the seraphim. 3 One called to another, and said,

"Holy, holy, holy, is Yahweh of Armies!
The whole earth is full of his glory!"

⁴ The foundations of the thresholds shook at the voice of him who called, and the house was filled with smoke. ⁵ Then I said, "Woe is me! For I am undone, because I am a man of unclean lips and I live among a people of unclean lips, for my eyes have seen the King, Yahweh of Armies!"

⁶ Then one of the seraphim flew to me, having a live coal in his hand, which he had taken with the tongs from off the altar. ⁷ He touched my mouth with it, and said, "Behold, this has touched your lips; and your iniquity is taken away, and your sin forgiven."

⁸ I heard the Lord's voice, saying, "Whom shall I send, and who will go for us?"
Then I said, "Here I am. Send me!"

Responsorial Psalm: Psalms 138: 1-5, 7c-8

¹ I will give you thanks with my whole heart.
Before the gods,⁺ I will sing praises to you.
² I will bow down toward your holy temple,
and give thanks to your Name for your loving kindness and for your truth;
for you have exalted your Name and your Word above all.
³ In the day that I called, you answered me.
You encouraged me with strength in my soul.
⁴ All the kings of the earth will give you thanks, Yahweh,
for they have heard the words of your mouth.
⁵ Yes, they will sing of the ways of Yahweh,
for Yahweh's glory is great!
⁷ᶜ Your right hand will save me.
⁸ Yahweh will fulfill that which concerns me.
Your loving kindness, Yahweh, endures forever.
Don't forsake the works of your own hands.

Second Reading: First Corinthians 15: 1-11

¹ Now I declare to you, brothers, the Good News which I preached to you, which also you received, in which you also stand, ² by which also you are saved, if you hold firmly the word which I preached to you—unless you believed in vain.

³ For I delivered to you first of all that which I also received: that Christ died for our sins according to the Scriptures, ⁴ that he was buried, that he was raised on the third day according to the Scriptures, ⁵ and that he appeared to Cephas, then to the twelve. ⁶ Then he appeared to over five hundred brothers at once, most of whom remain until now, but some have also fallen asleep. ⁷ Then he appeared to James, then to all the apostles, ⁸ and last of all, as to the child born at the wrong time, he appeared to me also. ⁹ For I am the least of the apostles, who is not worthy to be called an apostle, because I persecuted the assembly

of God. [10] But by the grace of God I am what I am. His grace which was given to me was not futile, but I worked more than all of them; yet not I, but the grace of God which was with me. [11] Whether then it is I or they, so we preach, and so you believed.

Gospel: Luke 5: 1-11

[1] Now while the multitude pressed on him and heard the word of God, he was standing by the lake of Gennesaret. [2] He saw two boats standing by the lake, but the fishermen had gone out of them and were washing their nets. [3] He entered into one of the boats, which was Simon's, and asked him to put out a little from the land. He sat down and taught the multitudes from the boat.

[4] When he had finished speaking, he said to Simon, "Put out into the deep and let down your nets for a catch."

[5] Simon answered him, "Master, we worked all night and caught nothing; but at your word I will let down the net." [6] When they had done this, they caught a great multitude of fish, and their net was breaking. [7] They beckoned to their partners in the other boat, that they should come and help them. They came and filled both boats, so that they began to sink. [8] But Simon Peter, when he saw it, fell down at Jesus' knees, saying, "Depart from me, for I am a sinful man, Lord." [9] For he was amazed, and all who were with him, at the catch of fish which they had caught; [10] and so also were James and John, sons of Zebedee, who were partners with Simon.

Jesus said to Simon, "Don't be afraid. From now on you will be catching people alive."

[11] When they had brought their boats to land, they left everything, and followed him.

1. Invite the Holy Spirit into this reading, asking the Author of Scripture to speak to you through His Word
2. Read today's passage as many times as you need, take your time
3. Write down (below) what the Lord is saying to you today
4. Live with this Word in your heart through the day

_____

_____

Sunday, February 16, 2025
SIXTH SUNDAY IN ORDINARY TIME

First Reading: Jeremiah 17: 5-8

5 Yahweh says:
"Cursed is the man who trusts in man,
relies on strength of flesh,
and whose heart departs from Yahweh.
6 For he will be like a bush in the desert,
and will not see when good comes,
but will inhabit the parched places in the wilderness,
an uninhabited salt land.
7 "Blessed is the man who trusts in Yahweh,
and whose confidence is in Yahweh.
8 For he will be as a tree planted by the waters,
who spreads out its roots by the river,
and will not fear when heat comes,
but its leaf will be green,
and will not be concerned in the year of drought.
It won't cease from yielding fruit.

Responsorial Psalm: Psalms 1: 1-4 and 6

1 Blessed is the man who doesn't walk in the counsel of the wicked,
nor stand on the path of sinners,
nor sit in the seat of scoffers;
2 but his delight is in Yahweh's law.
On his law he meditates day and night.
3 He will be like a tree planted by the streams of water,
that produces its fruit in its season,
whose leaf also does not wither.
Whatever he does shall prosper.
4 The wicked are not so,
but are like the chaff which the wind drives away.
6 For Yahweh knows the way of the righteous,
but the way of the wicked shall perish.

Second Reading: First Corinthians 15: 12, 16-20

12 Now if Christ is preached, that he has been raised from the dead, how do some among you say that there is no resurrection of the dead?
16 For if the dead aren't raised, neither has Christ been raised. 17 If Christ has not been raised, your faith is vain; you are still in your sins. 18 Then they also who are fallen asleep

in Christ have perished. ¹⁹ If we have only hoped in Christ in this life, we are of all men most pitiable.

²⁰ But now Christ has been raised from the dead. He became the first fruit of those who are asleep.

Gospel: Luke 6: 17, 20-26

¹⁷ He came down with them and stood on a level place, with a crowd of his disciples and a great number of the people from all Judea and Jerusalem and the sea coast of Tyre and Sidon, who came to hear him and to be healed of their diseases,

²⁰ He lifted up his eyes to his disciples, and said:

"Blessed are you who are poor,

for God's Kingdom is yours.

²¹ Blessed are you who hunger now,

for you will be filled.

Blessed are you who weep now,

for you will laugh.

²² Blessed are you when men hate you, and when they exclude and mock you, and throw out your name as evil, for the Son of Man's sake.

²³ Rejoice in that day and leap for joy, for behold, your reward is great in heaven, for their fathers did the same thing to the prophets.

²⁴ "But woe to you who are rich!

For you have received your consolation.

²⁵ Woe to you, you who are full now,

for you will be hungry.

Woe to you who laugh now,

for you will mourn and weep.

²⁶ Woe,‡ when‡ men speak well of you,

for their fathers did the same thing to the false prophets.

1. Invite the Holy Spirit into this reading, asking the Author of Scripture to speak to you through His Word

2. Read today's passage as many times as you need, take your time

3. Write down (below) what the Lord is saying to you today

4. Live with this Word in your heart through the day

_____

_____

First Reading: First Samuel 26: 2, 7-9, 12-13, 22-23

² Then Saul arose and went down to the wilderness of Ziph, having three thousand chosen men of Israel with him, to seek David in the wilderness of Ziph.

⁷ So David and Abishai came to the people by night; and, behold, Saul lay sleeping within the place of the wagons, with his spear stuck in the ground at his head; and Abner and the people lay around him. ⁸ Then Abishai said to David, "God has delivered up your enemy into your hand today. Now therefore please let me strike him with the spear to the earth at one stroke, and I will not strike him the second time."

⁹ David said to Abishai, "Don't destroy him, for who can stretch out his hand against Yahweh's anointed, and be guiltless?"

¹² So David took the spear and the jar of water from Saul's head, and they went away. No man saw it, or knew it, nor did any awake; for they were all asleep, because a deep sleep from Yahweh had fallen on them. ¹³ Then David went over to the other side, and stood on the top of the mountain far away, a great space being between them;

²² David answered, "Behold the spear, O king! Let one of the young men come over and get it. ²³ Yahweh will render to every man his righteousness and his faithfulness; because Yahweh delivered you into my hand today, and I wouldn't stretch out my hand against Yahweh's anointed.

Responsorial Psalm: Psalms 103: 1-4, 8, 10, 12-13

¹ Praise Yahweh, my soul!
All that is within me, praise his holy name!
² Praise Yahweh, my soul,
and don't forget all his benefits,
³ who forgives all your sins,
who heals all your diseases,
⁴ who redeems your life from destruction,
who crowns you with loving kindness and tender mercies,
⁸ Yahweh is merciful and gracious,
slow to anger, and abundant in loving kindness.
¹⁰ He has not dealt with us according to our sins,
nor repaid us for our iniquities.
¹² As far as the east is from the west,
so far has he removed our transgressions from us.
¹³ Like a father has compassion on his children,

so Yahweh has compassion on those who fear him.
Second Reading: First Corinthians 15: 45-49

[45] So also it is written, "The first man Adam became a living soul." [*] The last Adam became a life-giving spirit. [46] However, that which is spiritual isn't first, but that which is natural, then that which is spiritual. [47] The first man is of the earth, made of dust. The second man is the Lord from heaven. [48] As is the one made of dust, such are those who are also made of dust; and as is the heavenly, such are they also that are heavenly. [49] As we have borne the image of those made of dust, let's[‡] also bear the image of the heavenly.

Gospel: Luke 6: 27-38

[27] "But I tell you who hear: love your enemies, do good to those who hate you, [28] bless those who curse you, and pray for those who mistreat you. [29] To him who strikes you on the cheek, offer also the other; and from him who takes away your cloak, don't withhold your coat also. [30] Give to everyone who asks you, and don't ask him who takes away your goods to give them back again.
[31] "As you would like people to do to you, do exactly so to them.
[32] "If you love those who love you, what credit is that to you? For even sinners love those who love them. [33] If you do good to those who do good to you, what credit is that to you? For even sinners do the same. [34] If you lend to those from whom you hope to receive, what credit is that to you? Even sinners lend to sinners, to receive back as much. [35] But love your enemies, and do good, and lend, expecting nothing back; and your reward will be great, and you will be children of the Most High; for he is kind toward the unthankful and evil.
[36] "Therefore be merciful,
even as your Father is also merciful.
[37] Don't judge,
and you won't be judged.
Don't condemn,
and you won't be condemned.
Set free,
and you will be set free.
[38] "Give, and it will be given to you: good measure, pressed down, shaken together, and running over, will be given to you.[§] For with the same measure you measure it will be measured back to you."

1. Invite the Holy Spirit into this reading, asking the Author of Scripture to speak to you through His Word
2. Read today's passage as many times as you need, take your time
3. Write down (below) what the Lord is saying to you today

4. Live with this Word in your heart through the day

_____

_____

Sunday, March 2, 2025
EIGHTH SUNDAY IN ORDINARY TIME

First Reading: Sirach 27: 4-7

4 In the shaking of a sieve, the refuse remains,
so does the filth of man in his thoughts.
5 The furnace tests the potter's vessels;
so the test of a person is in his thoughts.
6 The fruit of a tree discloses its cultivation,
so is the utterance of the thought of a person's heart.
7 Praise no man before you hear his thoughts,
for this is how people are tested.

Responsorial Psalm: Psalms 92: 2-3, 13-15

2 to proclaim your loving kindness in the morning,
and your faithfulness every night,
3 with the ten-stringed lute, with the harp,
and with the melody of the lyre.
13 They are planted in Yahweh's house.
They will flourish in our God's courts.
14 They will still produce fruit in old age.
They will be full of sap and green,
15 to show that Yahweh is upright.
He is my rock,
and there is no unrighteousness in him.

Second Reading: First Corinthians 15: 54-58

54 But when this perishable body will have become imperishable, and this mortal will have put on immortality, then what is written will happen: "Death is swallowed up in victory."
55 "Death, where is your sting?

Hades,[±] where is your victory?"[*]

56 The sting of death is sin, and the power of sin is the law. 57 But thanks be to God, who gives us the victory through our Lord Jesus Christ. 58 Therefore, my beloved brothers, be steadfast, immovable, always abounding in the Lord's work, because you know that your labor is not in vain in the Lord.

Gospel: Luke 6: 39-45

39 He spoke a parable to them. "Can the blind guide the blind? Won't they both fall into a pit? 40 A disciple is not above his teacher, but everyone when he is fully trained will be like his teacher. 41 Why do you see the speck of chaff that is in your brother's eye, but don't consider the beam that is in your own eye? 42 Or how can you tell your brother, 'Brother, let me remove the speck of chaff that is in your eye,' when you yourself don't see the beam that is in your own eye? You hypocrite! First remove the beam from your own eye, and then you can see clearly to remove the speck of chaff that is in your brother's eye.

43 "For there is no good tree that produces rotten fruit, nor again a rotten tree that produces good fruit. 44 For each tree is known by its own fruit. For people don't gather figs from thorns, nor do they gather grapes from a bramble bush. 45 The good man out of the good treasure of his heart brings out that which is good, and the evil man out of the evil treasure of his heart brings out that which is evil, for out of the abundance of the heart, his mouth speaks.

1. Invite the Holy Spirit into this reading, asking the Author of Scripture to speak to you through His Word
2. Read today's passage as many times as you need, take your time
3. Write down (below) what the Lord is saying to you today
4. Live with this Word in your heart through the day

_____

_____

Wednesday, March 5, 2025
Ash Wednesday

First Reading: Joel 2: 12-18

12 "Yet even now," says Yahweh, "turn to me with all your heart,
and with fasting, and with weeping, and with mourning."

¹³ Tear your heart and not your garments,
and turn to Yahweh, your God;
for he is gracious and merciful,
slow to anger, and abundant in loving kindness,
and relents from sending calamity.
¹⁴ Who knows? He may turn and relent,
and leave a blessing behind him,
even a meal offering and a drink offering to Yahweh, your God.
¹⁵ Blow the trumpet in Zion!
Sanctify a fast.
Call a solemn assembly.
¹⁶ Gather the people.
Sanctify the assembly.
Assemble the elders.
Gather the children, and those who nurse from breasts.
Let the bridegroom go out of his room,
and the bride out of her chamber.
¹⁷ Let the priests, the ministers of Yahweh, weep between the porch and the altar,
and let them say, "Spare your people, Yahweh,
and don't give your heritage to reproach,
that the nations should rule over them.
Why should they say among the peoples,
'Where is their God?' "
¹⁸ Then Yahweh was jealous for his land,
and had pity on his people.

Responsorial Psalm: Psalms 51: 3-6ab, 12-14 and 17

³ For I know my transgressions.
My sin is constantly before me.
⁴ Against you, and you only, I have sinned,
and done that which is evil in your sight,
so you may be proved right when you speak,
and justified when you judge.
⁵ Behold, I was born in iniquity.
My mother conceived me in sin.
⁶ Behold, you desire truth in the inward parts.
You teach me wisdom in the inmost place.
¹² Restore to me the joy of your salvation.
Uphold me with a willing spirit.

¹³ Then I will teach transgressors your ways.

Sinners will be converted to you.

¹⁴ Deliver me from the guilt of bloodshed, O God, the God of my salvation.

My tongue will sing aloud of your righteousness.

¹⁷ The sacrifices of God are a broken spirit.

O God, you will not despise a broken and contrite heart.

Second Reading: Second Corinthians 5: 20 – 6:2

²⁰ We are therefore ambassadors on behalf of Christ, as though God were entreating by us: we beg you on behalf of Christ, be reconciled to God. ²¹ For him who knew no sin he made to be sin on our behalf, so that in him we might become the righteousness of God. ¹ Working together, we entreat also that you do not receive the grace of God in vain. ² For he says,

"At an acceptable time I listened to you.

In a day of salvation I helped you."*

Behold, now is the acceptable time. Behold, now is the day of salvation.

Gospel: Matthew 6: 1-6, 16-18

¹ "Be careful that you don't do your charitable giving⁺ before men, to be seen by them, or else you have no reward from your Father who is in heaven. ² Therefore, when you do merciful deeds, don't sound a trumpet before yourself, as the hypocrites do in the synagogues and in the streets, that they may get glory from men. Most certainly I tell you, they have received their reward. ³ But when you do merciful deeds, don't let your left hand know what your right hand does, ⁴ so that your merciful deeds may be in secret, then your Father who sees in secret will reward you openly.

⁵ "When you pray, you shall not be as the hypocrites, for they love to stand and pray in the synagogues and in the corners of the streets, that they may be seen by men. Most certainly, I tell you, they have received their reward. ⁶ But you, when you pray, enter into your inner room, and having shut your door, pray to your Father who is in secret; and your Father who sees in secret will reward you openly.

¹⁶ "Moreover when you fast, don't be like the hypocrites, with sad faces. For they disfigure their faces that they may be seen by men to be fasting. Most certainly I tell you, they have received their reward. ¹⁷ But you, when you fast, anoint your head and wash your face, ¹⁸ so that you are not seen by men to be fasting, but by your Father who is in secret; and your Father, who sees in secret, will reward you.

1. Invite the Holy Spirit into this reading, asking the Author of Scripture to speak to you through His Word

2. Read today's passage as many times as you need, take your time
3. Write down (below) what the Lord is saying to you today
4. Live with this Word in your heart through the day

Sunday, March 9, 2025
FIRST SUNDAY OF LENT

First Reading: Deuteronomy 26: 4-10

4 The priest shall take the basket out of your hand, and set it down before Yahweh your God's altar. 5 You shall answer and say before Yahweh your God, "My father† was a Syrian ready to perish. He went down into Egypt, and lived there, few in number. There he became a great, mighty, and populous nation. 6 The Egyptians mistreated us, afflicted us, and imposed hard labor on us. 7 Then we cried to Yahweh, the God of our fathers. Yahweh heard our voice, and saw our affliction, our toil, and our oppression. 8 Yahweh brought us out of Egypt with a mighty hand, with an outstretched arm, with great terror, with signs, and with wonders; 9 and he has brought us into this place, and has given us this land, a land flowing with milk and honey. 10 Now, behold, I have brought the first of the fruit of the ground, which you, Yahweh, have given me." You shall set it down before Yahweh your God, and worship before Yahweh your God.

Responsorial Psalm: Psalms 91: 1-2, 10-15

1 He who dwells in the secret place of the Most High
will rest in the shadow of the Almighty.
2 I will say of Yahweh, "He is my refuge and my fortress;
my God, in whom I trust."
10 no evil shall happen to you,
neither shall any plague come near your dwelling.
11 For he will put his angels in charge of you,
to guard you in all your ways.
12 They will bear you up in their hands,
so that you won't dash your foot against a stone.
13 You will tread on the lion and cobra.
You will trample the young lion and the serpent underfoot.

¹⁴ "Because he has set his love on me, therefore I will deliver him.
I will set him on high, because he has known my name.
¹⁵ He will call on me, and I will answer him.
I will be with him in trouble.
I will deliver him, and honor him.

Second Reading: Romans 10: 8-13

⁸ But what does it say? "The word is near you, in your mouth and in your heart;"* that is, the word of faith which we preach: ⁹ that if you will confess with your mouth that Jesus is Lord and believe in your heart that God raised him from the dead, you will be saved. ¹⁰ For with the heart one believes resulting in righteousness; and with the mouth confession is made resulting in salvation. ¹¹ For the Scripture says, "Whoever believes in him will not be disappointed."*
¹² For there is no distinction between Jew and Greek; for the same Lord is Lord of all, and is rich to all who call on him. ¹³ For, "Whoever will call on the name of the Lord will be saved."

Gospel: Luke 4: 1-13

¹ Jesus, full of the Holy Spirit, returned from the Jordan and was led by the Spirit into the wilderness ² for forty days, being tempted by the devil. He ate nothing in those days. Afterward, when they were completed, he was hungry.
³ The devil said to him, "If you are the Son of God, command this stone to become bread."
⁴ Jesus answered him, saying, "It is written, 'Man shall not live by bread alone, but by every word of God.' "*
⁵ The devil, leading him up on a high mountain, showed him all the kingdoms of the world in a moment of time. ⁶ The devil said to him, "I will give you all this authority and their glory, for it has been delivered to me, and I give it to whomever I want. ⁷ If you therefore will worship before me, it will all be yours."
⁸ Jesus answered him, "Get behind me, Satan! For it is written, 'You shall worship the Lord your God, and you shall serve him only.' "*
⁹ He led him to Jerusalem and set him on the pinnacle of the temple, and said to him, "If you are the Son of God, cast yourself down from here, ¹⁰ for it is written,
'He will put his angels in charge of you, to guard you;'
¹¹ and,
'On their hands they will bear you up,
lest perhaps you dash your foot against a stone.' "*
¹² Jesus answering, said to him, "It has been said, 'You shall not tempt the Lord your God.' "*

¹³ When the devil had completed every temptation, he departed from him until another time.

1. Invite the Holy Spirit into this reading, asking the Author of Scripture to speak to you through His Word
2. Read today's passage as many times as you need, take your time
3. Write down (below) what the Lord is saying to you today
4. Live with this Word in your heart through the day

Sunday, March 16, 2025
SECOND SUNDAY OF LENT

First Reading: Genesis 15: 5-12, 17-18

⁵ Yahweh brought him outside, and said, "Look now toward the sky, and count the stars, if you are able to count them." He said to Abram, "So your offspring will be." ⁶ He believed in Yahweh, who credited it to him for righteousness. ⁷ He said to Abram, "I am Yahweh who brought you out of Ur of the Chaldees, to give you this land to inherit it."
⁸ He said, "Lord Yahweh, how will I know that I will inherit it?"
⁹ He said to him, "Bring me a heifer three years old, a female goat three years old, a ram three years old, a turtledove, and a young pigeon." ¹⁰ He brought him all these, and divided them in the middle, and laid each half opposite the other; but he didn't divide the birds. ¹¹ The birds of prey came down on the carcasses, and Abram drove them away.
¹² When the sun was going down, a deep sleep fell on Abram. Now terror and great darkness fell on him.
¹⁷ It came to pass that, when the sun went down, and it was dark, behold, a smoking furnace and a flaming torch passed between these pieces. ¹⁸ In that day Yahweh made a covenant with Abram, saying, "I have given this land to your offspring, from the river of Egypt to the great river, the river Euphrates:

Responsorial Psalm: Psalms 27: 1, 7-9, 13-14

¹ Yahweh is my light and my salvation.
Whom shall I fear?
Yahweh is the strength of my life.

Of whom shall I be afraid?
7 Hear, Yahweh, when I cry with my voice.
Have mercy also on me, and answer me.
8 When you said, "Seek my face,"
my heart said to you, "I will seek your face, Yahweh."
9 Don't hide your face from me.
Don't put your servant away in anger.
You have been my help.
Don't abandon me,
neither forsake me, God of my salvation.
13 I am still confident of this:
I will see the goodness of Yahweh in the land of the living.
14 Wait for Yahweh.
Be strong, and let your heart take courage.
Yes, wait for Yahweh.

Second Reading: Philippians 3: 17 – 4: 1

17 Brothers, be imitators together of me, and note those who walk this way, even as you have us for an example. 18 For many walk, of whom I told you often, and now tell you even weeping, as the enemies of the cross of Christ, 19 whose end is destruction, whose god is the belly, and whose glory is in their shame, who think about earthly things. 20 For our citizenship is in heaven, from where we also wait for a Savior, the Lord Jesus Christ, 21 who will change the body of our humiliation to be conformed to the body of his glory, according to the working by which he is able even to subject all things to himself.
1 Therefore, my brothers, beloved and longed for, my joy and crown, stand firm in the Lord in this way, my beloved.

Gospel: Luke 9: 28-36

28 About eight days after these sayings, he took with him Peter, John, and James, and went up onto the mountain to pray. 29 As he was praying, the appearance of his face was altered, and his clothing became white and dazzling. 30 Behold, two men were talking with him, who were Moses and Elijah, 31 who appeared in glory and spoke of his departure, which he was about to accomplish at Jerusalem.
32 Now Peter and those who were with him were heavy with sleep, but when they were fully awake, they saw his glory, and the two men who stood with him. 33 As they were parting from him, Peter said to Jesus, "Master, it is good for us to be here. Let's make three tents: one for you, one for Moses, and one for Elijah," not knowing what he said.

34 While he said these things, a cloud came and overshadowed them, and they were afraid as they entered into the cloud. 35 A voice came out of the cloud, saying, "This is my beloved Son. Listen to him!" 36 When the voice came, Jesus was found alone. They were silent, and told no one in those days any of the things which they had seen.

1. Invite the Holy Spirit into this reading, asking the Author of Scripture to speak to you through His Word
2. Read today's passage as many times as you need, take your time
3. Write down (below) what the Lord is saying to you today
4. Live with this Word in your heart through the day

_____

_____

Sunday, March 23, 2025
THIRD SUNDAY OF LENT

First Reading: Exodus 3: 1-8a, 13-15

1 Now Moses was keeping the flock of Jethro, his father-in-law, the priest of Midian, and he led the flock to the back of the wilderness, and came to God's mountain, to Horeb. 2 Yahweh's‡ angel appeared to him in a flame of fire out of the middle of a bush. He looked, and behold, the bush burned with fire, and the bush was not consumed. 3 Moses said, "I will go now, and see this great sight, why the bush is not burned."
4 When Yahweh saw that he came over to see, God called to him out of the middle of the bush, and said, "Moses! Moses!"
He said, "Here I am."
5 He said, "Don't come close. Take off your sandals, for the place you are standing on is holy ground." 6 Moreover he said, "I am the God of your father, the God of Abraham, the God of Isaac, and the God of Jacob."
Moses hid his face because he was afraid to look at God.
7 Yahweh said, "I have surely seen the affliction of my people who are in Egypt, and have heard their cry because of their taskmasters, for I know their sorrows. 8 I have come down to deliver them out of the hand of the Egyptians, and to bring them up out of that land to a good and large land, to a land flowing with milk and honey;
13 Moses said to God, "Behold, when I come to the children of Israel, and tell them, 'The God of your fathers has sent me to you,' and they ask me, 'What is his name?' what should I tell them?"

¹⁴ God said to Moses, "I AM WHO I AM," and he said, "You shall tell the children of Israel this: 'I AM has sent me to you.' " ¹⁵ God said moreover to Moses, "You shall tell the children of Israel this, 'Yahweh, the God of your fathers, the God of Abraham, the God of Isaac, and the God of Jacob, has sent me to you.' This is my name forever, and this is my memorial to all generations.

Responsorial Psalm: Psalms 103: 1-4, 6-8, 11

¹ Praise Yahweh, my soul!
All that is within me, praise his holy name!
² Praise Yahweh, my soul,
and don't forget all his benefits,
³ who forgives all your sins,
who heals all your diseases,
⁴ who redeems your life from destruction,
who crowns you with loving kindness and tender mercies,
⁶ Yahweh executes righteous acts,
and justice for all who are oppressed.
⁷ He made known his ways to Moses,
his deeds to the children of Israel.
⁸ Yahweh is merciful and gracious,
slow to anger, and abundant in loving kindness.
¹¹ For as the heavens are high above the earth,
so great is his loving kindness toward those who fear him.

Second Reading: First Corinthians 10: 1-6, 10-12

¹ Now I would not have you ignorant, brothers, that our fathers were all under the cloud, and all passed through the sea; ² and were all baptized into Moses in the cloud and in the sea; ³ and all ate the same spiritual food; ⁴ and all drank the same spiritual drink. For they drank of a spiritual rock that followed them, and the rock was Christ. ⁵ However with most of them, God was not well pleased, for they were overthrown in the wilderness.
⁶ Now these things were our examples, to the intent we should not lust after evil things as they also lusted.
¹⁰ Don't grumble, as some of them also grumbled, and perished by the destroyer. ¹¹ Now all these things happened to them by way of example, and they were written for our admonition, on whom the ends of the ages have come. ¹² Therefore let him who thinks he stands be careful that he doesn't fall.

Gospel: Luke 13: 1-9

¹ Now there were some present at the same time who told him about the Galileans whose blood Pilate had mixed with their sacrifices. ² Jesus answered them, "Do you think that these Galileans were worse sinners than all the other Galileans, because they suffered such things? ³ I tell you, no, but unless you repent, you will all perish in the same way. ⁴ Or those eighteen on whom the tower in Siloam fell and killed them—do you think that they were worse offenders than all the men who dwell in Jerusalem? ⁵ I tell you, no, but, unless you repent, you will all perish in the same way."

⁶ He spoke this parable. "A certain man had a fig tree planted in his vineyard, and he came seeking fruit on it and found none. ⁷ He said to the vine dresser, 'Behold, these three years I have come looking for fruit on this fig tree, and found none. Cut it down! Why does it waste the soil?' ⁸ He answered, 'Lord, leave it alone this year also, until I dig around it and fertilize it. ⁹ If it bears fruit, fine; but if not, after that, you can cut it down.' "

1. Invite the Holy Spirit into this reading, asking the Author of Scripture to speak to you through His Word
2. Read today's passage as many times as you need, take your time
3. Write down (below) what the Lord is saying to you today
4. Live with this Word in your heart through the day

_____

_____

Sunday, March 30, 2025
FOURTH SUNDAY OF LENT

First Reading: Joshua 5: 9a, 10-12

⁹ Yahweh said to Joshua, "Today I have rolled away the reproach of Egypt from you." Therefore the name of that place was called Gilgal⁺ to this day. ¹⁰ The children of Israel encamped in Gilgal. They kept the Passover on the fourteenth day of the month at evening in the plains of Jericho. ¹¹ They ate unleavened cakes and parched grain of the produce of the land on the next day after the Passover, in the same day. ¹² The manna ceased on the next day, after they had eaten of the produce of the land. The children of Israel didn't have manna any more, but they ate of the fruit of the land of Canaan that year.

Responsorial Psalm: Psalms 34: 2-7

² My soul shall boast in Yahweh.
The humble shall hear of it and be glad.
³ Oh magnify Yahweh with me.
Let's exalt his name together.
⁴ I sought Yahweh, and he answered me,
and delivered me from all my fears.
⁵ They looked to him, and were radiant.
Their faces shall never be covered with shame.
⁶ This poor man cried, and Yahweh heard him,
and saved him out of all his troubles.
⁷ Yahweh's angel encamps around those who fear him,
and delivers them.

Second Reading: Second Corinthians 5: 17-21

¹⁷ Therefore if anyone is in Christ, he is a new creation. The old things have passed away. Behold,‡ all things have become new. ¹⁸ But all things are of God, who reconciled us to himself through Jesus Christ, and gave to us the ministry of reconciliation; ¹⁹ namely, that God was in Christ reconciling the world to himself, not reckoning to them their trespasses, and having committed to us the word of reconciliation.
²⁰ We are therefore ambassadors on behalf of Christ, as though God were entreating by us: we beg you on behalf of Christ, be reconciled to God. ²¹ For him who knew no sin he made to be sin on our behalf, so that in him we might become the righteousness of God.

Gospel: Luke 15: 1-3,11-32

¹ Now all the tax collectors and sinners were coming close to him to hear him. ² The Pharisees and the scribes murmured, saying, "This man welcomes sinners, and eats with them."
³ He told them this parable
¹¹ He said, "A certain man had two sons. ¹² The younger of them said to his father, 'Father, give me my share of your property.' So he divided his livelihood between them. ¹³ Not many days after, the younger son gathered all of this together and traveled into a far country. There he wasted his property with riotous living. ¹⁴ When he had spent all of it, there arose a severe famine in that country, and he began to be in need. ¹⁵ He went and joined himself to one of the citizens of that country, and he sent him into his fields to feed pigs. ¹⁶ He wanted to fill his belly with the pods that the pigs ate, but no one gave him any. ¹⁷ But when he came to himself, he said, 'How many hired servants of my father's have bread enough to spare, and I'm dying with hunger! ¹⁸ I will get up and go to my father, and will tell him,

"Father, I have sinned against heaven and in your sight. ¹⁹ I am no more worthy to be called your son. Make me as one of your hired servants." '

²⁰ "He arose and came to his father. But while he was still far off, his father saw him and was moved with compassion, and ran, fell on his neck, and kissed him. ²¹ The son said to him, 'Father, I have sinned against heaven and in your sight. I am no longer worthy to be called your son.'

²² "But the father said to his servants, 'Bring out the best robe and put it on him. Put a ring on his hand and sandals on his feet. ²³ Bring the fattened calf, kill it, and let's eat and celebrate; ²⁴ for this, my son, was dead and is alive again. He was lost and is found.' Then they began to celebrate.

²⁵ "Now his elder son was in the field. As he came near to the house, he heard music and dancing. ²⁶ He called one of the servants to him and asked what was going on. ²⁷ He said to him, 'Your brother has come, and your father has killed the fattened calf, because he has received him back safe and healthy.' ²⁸ But he was angry and would not go in. Therefore his father came out and begged him. ²⁹ But he answered his father, 'Behold, these many years I have served you, and I never disobeyed a commandment of yours, but you never gave me a goat, that I might celebrate with my friends. ³⁰ But when this your son came, who has devoured your living with prostitutes, you killed the fattened calf for him.'

³¹ "He said to him, 'Son, you are always with me, and all that is mine is yours. ³² But it was appropriate to celebrate and be glad, for this, your brother, was dead, and is alive again. He was lost, and is found.' "

1. Invite the Holy Spirit into this reading, asking the Author of Scripture to speak to you through His Word
2. Read today's passage as many times as you need, take your time
3. Write down (below) what the Lord is saying to you today
4. Live with this Word in your heart through the day

_____

_____

Sunday, April 6, 2025
FIFTH SUNDAY OF LENT

First Reading: Isaiah 43: 16-21

¹⁶ Yahweh, who makes a way in the sea,
and a path in the mighty waters,

¹⁷ who brings out the chariot and horse,
the army and the mighty man
(they lie down together, they shall not rise;
they are extinct, they are quenched like a wick) says:
¹⁸ "Don't remember the former things,
and don't consider the things of old.
¹⁹ Behold, I will do a new thing.
It springs out now.
Don't you know it?
I will even make a way in the wilderness,
and rivers in the desert.
²⁰ The animals of the field, the jackals and the ostriches, shall honor me,
because I give water in the wilderness and rivers in the desert,
to give drink to my people, my chosen,
²¹ the people which I formed for myself,
that they might declare my praise.

Responsorial Psalm: Psalms 126: 1-6

¹ When Yahweh brought back those who returned to Zion,
we were like those who dream.
² Then our mouth was filled with laughter,
and our tongue with singing.
Then they said among the nations,
"Yahweh has done great things for them."
³ Yahweh has done great things for us,
and we are glad.
⁴ Restore our fortunes again, Yahweh,
like the streams in the Negev.
⁵ Those who sow in tears will reap in joy.
⁶ He who goes out weeping, carrying seed for sowing,
will certainly come again with joy, carrying his sheaves.

Second Reading: Philippians 3: 8-14

⁸ Yes most certainly, and I count all things to be a loss for the excellency of the knowledge of Christ Jesus, my Lord, for whom I suffered the loss of all things, and count them nothing but refuse, that I may gain Christ ⁹ and be found in him, not having a righteousness of my own, that which is of the law, but that which is through faith in Christ, the righteousness which is from God by faith, ¹⁰ that I may know him and the power of his resurrection, and

the fellowship of his sufferings, becoming conformed to his death, ¹¹ if by any means I may attain to the resurrection from the dead. ¹² Not that I have already obtained, or am already made perfect; but I press on, that I may take hold of that for which also I was taken hold of by Christ Jesus.

¹³ Brothers, I don't regard myself as yet having taken hold, but one thing I do: forgetting the things which are behind and stretching forward to the things which are before, ¹⁴ I press on toward the goal for the prize of the high calling of God in Christ Jesus.

Gospel: John 8: 1-11

¹ but Jesus went to the Mount of Olives.

² Now very early in the morning, he came again into the temple, and all the people came to him. He sat down and taught them. ³ The scribes and the Pharisees brought a woman taken in adultery. Having set her in the middle, ⁴ they told him, "Teacher, we found this woman in adultery, in the very act. ⁵ Now in our law, Moses commanded us to stone such women.⋅ What then do you say about her?" ⁶ They said this testing him, that they might have something to accuse him of.

But Jesus stooped down and wrote on the ground with his finger. ⁷ But when they continued asking him, he looked up and said to them, "He who is without sin among you, let him throw the first stone at her." ⁸ Again he stooped down and wrote on the ground with his finger.

⁹ They, when they heard it, being convicted by their conscience, went out one by one, beginning from the oldest, even to the last. Jesus was left alone with the woman where she was, in the middle. ¹⁰ Jesus, standing up, saw her and said, "Woman, where are your accusers? Did no one condemn you?"

¹¹ She said, "No one, Lord."

Jesus said, "Neither do I condemn you. Go your way. From now on, sin no more."

1. Invite the Holy Spirit into this reading, asking the Author of Scripture to speak to you through His Word
2. Read today's passage as many times as you need, take your time
3. Write down (below) what the Lord is saying to you today
4. Live with this Word in your heart through the day

_____

_____

Sunday, April 13, 2025
PALM SUNDAY OF THE PASSION OF THE LORD

Procession: Luke 19: 28-40

28 Having said these things, he went on ahead, going up to Jerusalem.
29 When he came near to Bethsphage‡ and Bethany, at the mountain that is called Olivet, he sent two of his disciples, 30 saying, "Go your way into the village on the other side, in which, as you enter, you will find a colt tied, which no man has ever sat upon. Untie it and bring it. 31 If anyone asks you, 'Why are you untying it?' say to him: 'The Lord needs it.' "
32 Those who were sent went away and found things just as he had told them. 33 As they were untying the colt, its owners said to them, "Why are you untying the colt?" 34 They said, "The Lord needs it." 35 Then they brought it to Jesus. They threw their cloaks on the colt and sat Jesus on them. 36 As he went, they spread their cloaks on the road.
37 As he was now getting near, at the descent of the Mount of Olives, the whole multitude of the disciples began to rejoice and praise God with a loud voice for all the mighty works which they had seen, 38 saying, "Blessed is the King who comes in the name of the Lord! * Peace in heaven, and glory in the highest!"
39 Some of the Pharisees from the multitude said to him, "Teacher, rebuke your disciples!"
40 He answered them, "I tell you that if these were silent, the stones would cry out."

First Reading: Isaiah 50: 4-7

4 The Lord Yahweh has given me the tongue of those who are taught,
that I may know how to sustain with words him who is weary.
He awakens morning by morning,
he awakens my ear to hear as those who are taught.
5 The Lord Yahweh has opened my ear.
I was not rebellious.
I have not turned back.
6 I gave my back to those who beat me,
and my cheeks to those who plucked off the hair.
I didn't hide my face from shame and spitting.
7 For the Lord Yahweh will help me.
Therefore I have not been confounded.
Therefore I have set my face like a flint,
and I know that I won't be disappointed.

Responsorial Psalm: Psalms 22: 8-9, 17-20, 23-24

8 "He trusts in Yahweh.

Let him deliver him.

Let him rescue him, since he delights in him."

9 But you brought me out of the womb.

You made me trust while at my mother's breasts.

17 I can count all of my bones.

They look and stare at me.

18 They divide my garments among them.

They cast lots for my clothing.

19 But don't be far off, Yahweh.

You are my help. Hurry to help me!

20 Deliver my soul from the sword,

my precious life from the power of the dog.

23 You who fear Yahweh, praise him!

All you descendants of Jacob, glorify him!

Stand in awe of him, all you descendants of Israel!

24 For he has not despised nor abhorred the affliction of the afflicted,

neither has he hidden his face from him;

but when he cried to him, he heard.

Second Reading: Philippians 2:6-11

6 who, existing in the form of God, didn't consider equality with God a thing to be grasped, 7 but emptied himself, taking the form of a servant, being made in the likeness of men. 8 And being found in human form, he humbled himself, becoming obedient to the point of death, yes, the death of the cross. 9 Therefore God also highly exalted him, and gave to him the name which is above every name, 10 that at the name of Jesus every knee should bow, of those in heaven, those on earth, and those under the earth, 11 and that every tongue should confess that Jesus Christ is Lord, to the glory of God the Father.

Gospel: Luke 22: 14 – 23: 56

14 When the hour had come, he sat down with the twelve apostles. 15 He said to them, "I have earnestly desired to eat this Passover with you before I suffer, 16 for I tell you, I will no longer by any means eat of it until it is fulfilled in God's Kingdom." 17 He received a cup, and when he had given thanks, he said, "Take this and share it among yourselves, 18 for I tell you, I will not drink at all again from the fruit of the vine, until God's Kingdom comes." 19 He took bread, and when he had given thanks, he broke and gave it to them, saying, "This is my body which is given for you. Do this in memory of me." 20 Likewise, he took the cup after supper, saying, "This cup is the new covenant in my blood, which is poured out for

you. 21 But behold, the hand of him who betrays me is with me on the table. 22 The Son of Man indeed goes as it has been determined, but woe to that man through whom he is betrayed!"

23 They began to question among themselves which of them it was who would do this thing.

24 A dispute also arose among them, which of them was considered to be greatest. 25 He said to them, "The kings of the nations lord it over them, and those who have authority over them are called 'benefactors.' 26 But not so with you. Rather, the one who is greater among you, let him become as the younger, and one who is governing, as one who serves. 27 For who is greater, one who sits at the table, or one who serves? Isn't it he who sits at the table? But I am among you as one who serves.

28 "But you are those who have continued with me in my trials. 29 I confer on you a kingdom, even as my Father conferred on me, 30 that you may eat and drink at my table in my Kingdom. You will sit on thrones, judging the twelve tribes of Israel."

31 The Lord said, "Simon, Simon, behold, Satan asked to have all of you, that he might sift you as wheat, 32 but I prayed for you, that your faith wouldn't fail. You, when once you have turned again, establish your brothers."†

33 He said to him, "Lord, I am ready to go with you both to prison and to death!"

34 He said, "I tell you, Peter, the rooster will by no means crow today until you deny that you know me three times."

35 He said to them, "When I sent you out without purse, bag, and sandals, did you lack anything?"

They said, "Nothing."

36 Then he said to them, "But now, whoever has a purse, let him take it, and likewise a bag. Whoever has none, let him sell his cloak, and buy a sword. 37 For I tell you that this which is written must still be fulfilled in me: 'He was counted with transgressors.'‡ For that which concerns me is being fulfilled."

38 They said, "Lord, behold, here are two swords."

He said to them, "That is enough."

39 He came out and went, as his custom was, to the Mount of Olives. His disciples also followed him. 40 When he was at the place, he said to them, "Pray that you don't enter into temptation."

41 He was withdrawn from them about a stone's throw, and he knelt down and prayed, 42 saying, "Father, if you are willing, remove this cup from me. Nevertheless, not my will, but yours, be done."

43 An angel from heaven appeared to him, strengthening him. 44 Being in agony, he prayed more earnestly. His sweat became like great drops of blood falling down on the ground.

45 When he rose up from his prayer, he came to the disciples and found them sleeping because of grief, 46 and said to them, "Why do you sleep? Rise and pray that you may not enter into temptation."

47 While he was still speaking, a crowd appeared. He who was called Judas, one of the twelve, was leading them. He came near to Jesus to kiss him. 48 But Jesus said to him, "Judas, do you betray the Son of Man with a kiss?"

49 When those who were around him saw what was about to happen, they said to him, "Lord, shall we strike with the sword?" 50 A certain one of them struck the servant of the high priest, and cut off his right ear.

51 But Jesus answered, "Let me at least do this"—and he touched his ear and healed him. 52 Jesus said to the chief priests, captains of the temple, and elders, who had come against him, "Have you come out as against a robber, with swords and clubs? 53 When I was with you in the temple daily, you didn't stretch out your hands against me. But this is your hour, and the power of darkness."

54 They seized him and led him away, and brought him into the high priest's house. But Peter followed from a distance. 55 When they had kindled a fire in the middle of the courtyard and had sat down together, Peter sat among them. 56 A certain servant girl saw him as he sat in the light, and looking intently at him, said, "This man also was with him."

57 He denied Jesus, saying, "Woman, I don't know him."

58 After a little while someone else saw him and said, "You also are one of them!"

But Peter answered, "Man, I am not!"

59 After about one hour passed, another confidently affirmed, saying, "Truly this man also was with him, for he is a Galilean!"

60 But Peter said, "Man, I don't know what you are talking about!" Immediately, while he was still speaking, a rooster crowed. 61 The Lord turned and looked at Peter. Then Peter remembered the Lord's word, how he said to him, "Before the rooster crows you will deny me three times." 62 He went out, and wept bitterly.

63 The men who held Jesus mocked him and beat him. 64 Having blindfolded him, they struck him on the face and asked him, "Prophesy! Who is the one who struck you?" 65 They spoke many other things against him, insulting him.

66 As soon as it was day, the assembly of the elders of the people were gathered together, both chief priests and scribes, and they led him away into their council, saying, 67 "If you are the Christ, tell us."

But he said to them, "If I tell you, you won't believe, 68 and if I ask, you will in no way answer me or let me go. 69 From now on, the Son of Man will be seated at the right hand of the power of God."

70 They all said, "Are you then the Son of God?"

He said to them, "You say it, because I am."

71 They said, "Why do we need any more witness? For we ourselves have heard from his own mouth!"

1 The whole company of them rose up and brought him before Pilate. 2 They began to accuse him, saying, "We found this man perverting the nation, forbidding paying taxes to Caesar, and saying that he himself is Christ, a king."

3 Pilate asked him, "Are you the King of the Jews?"

He answered him, "So you say."

4 Pilate said to the chief priests and the multitudes, "I find no basis for a charge against this man."

5 But they insisted, saying, "He stirs up the people, teaching throughout all Judea, beginning from Galilee even to this place."

6 But when Pilate heard Galilee mentioned, he asked if the man was a Galilean. 7 When he found out that he was in Herod's jurisdiction, he sent him to Herod, who was also in Jerusalem during those days.

8 Now when Herod saw Jesus, he was exceedingly glad, for he had wanted to see him for a long time, because he had heard many things about him. He hoped to see some miracle done by him. 9 He questioned him with many words, but he gave no answers. 10 The chief priests and the scribes stood, vehemently accusing him. 11 Herod with his soldiers humiliated him and mocked him. Dressing him in luxurious clothing, they sent him back to Pilate. 12 Herod and Pilate became friends with each other that very day, for before that they were enemies with each other.

13 Pilate called together the chief priests, the rulers, and the people, 14 and said to them, "You brought this man to me as one that perverts the people, and behold, having examined him before you, I found no basis for a charge against this man concerning those things of which you accuse him. 15 Neither has Herod, for I sent you to him, and see, nothing worthy of death has been done by him. 16 I will therefore chastise him and release him."

17 Now he had to release one prisoner to them at the feast.‡ 18 But they all cried out together, saying, "Away with this man! Release to us Barabbas!"— 19 one who was thrown into prison for a certain revolt in the city, and for murder.

20 Then Pilate spoke to them again, wanting to release Jesus, 21 but they shouted, saying, "Crucify! Crucify him!"

22 He said to them the third time, "Why? What evil has this man done? I have found no capital crime in him. I will therefore chastise him and release him." 23 But they were urgent with loud voices, asking that he might be crucified. Their voices and the voices of the chief priests prevailed. 24 Pilate decreed that what they asked for should be done. 25 He released him who had been thrown into prison for insurrection and murder, for whom they asked, but he delivered Jesus up to their will.

26 When they led him away, they grabbed one Simon of Cyrene, coming from the country, and laid the cross on him to carry it after Jesus. 27 A great multitude of the people followed him, including women who also mourned and lamented him. 28 But Jesus, turning to them, said, "Daughters of Jerusalem, don't weep for me, but weep for yourselves and for your children. 29 For behold, the days are coming in which they will say, 'Blessed are the barren, the wombs that never bore, and the breasts that never nursed.' 30 Then they will begin to tell the mountains, 'Fall on us!' and tell the hills, 'Cover us.'* 31 For if they do these things in the green tree, what will be done in the dry?"

32 There were also others, two criminals, led with him to be put to death. 33 When they came to the place that is called "The Skull", they crucified him there with the criminals, one on the right and the other on the left.

34 Jesus said, "Father, forgive them, for they don't know what they are doing."

Dividing his garments among them, they cast lots. 35 The people stood watching. The rulers with them also scoffed at him, saying, "He saved others. Let him save himself, if this is the Christ of God, his chosen one!"

36 The soldiers also mocked him, coming to him and offering him vinegar, 37 and saying, "If you are the King of the Jews, save yourself!"

38 An inscription was also written over him in letters of Greek, Latin, and Hebrew: "THIS IS THE KING OF THE JEWS."

39 One of the criminals who was hanged insulted him, saying, "If you are the Christ, save yourself and us!"

40 But the other answered, and rebuking him said, "Don't you even fear God, seeing you are under the same condemnation? 41 And we indeed justly, for we receive the due reward for our deeds, but this man has done nothing wrong." 42 He said to Jesus, "Lord, remember me when you come into your Kingdom."

43 Jesus said to him, "Assuredly I tell you, today you will be with me in Paradise."

44 It was now about the sixth hour,‡ and darkness came over the whole land until the ninth hour.§ 45 The sun was darkened, and the veil of the temple was torn in two. 46 Jesus, crying with a loud voice, said, "Father, into your hands I commit my spirit!" Having said this, he breathed his last.

47 When the centurion saw what was done, he glorified God, saying, "Certainly this was a righteous man." 48 All the multitudes that came together to see this, when they saw the things that were done, returned home beating their chests. 49 All his acquaintances and the women who followed with him from Galilee stood at a distance, watching these things.

50 Behold, there was a man named Joseph, who was a member of the council, a good and righteous man 51 (he had not consented to their counsel and deed), from Arimathaea, a city of the Jews, who was also waiting for God's Kingdom. 52 This man went to Pilate, and asked for Jesus' body. 53 He took it down and wrapped it in a linen cloth, and laid him in a tomb that was cut in stone, where no one had ever been laid. 54 It was the day of the Preparation, and the Sabbath was drawing near. 55 The women who had come with him out of Galilee followed after, and saw the tomb and how his body was laid. 56 They returned and prepared spices and ointments. On the Sabbath they rested according to the commandment.

1. Invite the Holy Spirit into this reading, asking the Author of Scripture to speak to you through His Word
2. Read today's passage as many times as you need, take your time
3. Write down (below) what the Lord is saying to you today
4. Live with this Word in your heart through the day

Thursday, April 17, 2025
Thursday of Holy Week (Holy Thursday)

First Reading: Exodus 12: 1-8, 11-14

¹ Yahweh spoke to Moses and Aaron in the land of Egypt, saying, ² "This month shall be to you the beginning of months. It shall be the first month of the year to you. ³ Speak to all the congregation of Israel, saying, 'On the tenth day of this month, they shall take to them every man a lamb, according to their fathers' houses, a lamb for a household; ⁴ and if the household is too little for a lamb, then he and his neighbor next to his house shall take one according to the number of the souls. You shall make your count for the lamb according to what everyone can eat. ⁵ Your lamb shall be without defect, a male a year old. You shall take it from the sheep or from the goats. ⁶ You shall keep it until the fourteenth day of the same month; and the whole assembly of the congregation of Israel shall kill it at evening. ⁷ They shall take some of the blood, and put it on the two door posts and on the lintel, on the houses in which they shall eat it. ⁸ They shall eat the meat in that night, roasted with fire, with unleavened bread. They shall eat it with bitter herbs.

¹¹ This is how you shall eat it: with your belt on your waist, your sandals on your feet, and your staff in your hand; and you shall eat it in haste: it is Yahweh's Passover. ¹² For I will go through the land of Egypt in that night, and will strike all the firstborn in the land of Egypt, both man and animal. I will execute judgments against all the gods of Egypt. I am Yahweh. ¹³ The blood shall be to you for a token on the houses where you are. When I see the blood, I will pass over you, and no plague will be on you to destroy you when I strike the land of Egypt. ¹⁴ This day shall be a memorial for you. You shall keep it as a feast to Yahweh. You shall keep it as a feast throughout your generations by an ordinance forever.

Responsorial Psalm: Psalms 116: 12-13, 15-18

¹² What will I give to Yahweh for all his benefits toward me?
¹³ I will take the cup of salvation, and call on Yahweh's name.
¹⁵ Precious in Yahweh's sight is the death of his saints.
¹⁶ Yahweh, truly I am your servant.
I am your servant, the son of your servant girl.
You have freed me from my chains.

17 I will offer to you the sacrifice of thanksgiving,
and will call on Yahweh's name.
18 I will pay my vows to Yahweh,
yes, in the presence of all his people,

Second Reading: First Corinthians 11: 23-26

23 For I received from the Lord that which also I delivered to you, that the Lord Jesus on the night in which he was betrayed took bread. 24 When he had given thanks, he broke it and said, "Take, eat. This is my body, which is broken for you. Do this in memory of me." 25 In the same way he also took the cup after supper, saying, "This cup is the new covenant in my blood. Do this, as often as you drink, in memory of me." 26 For as often as you eat this bread and drink this cup, you proclaim the Lord's death until he comes.

Gospel: John 13: 1-15

1 Now before the feast of the Passover, Jesus, knowing that his time had come that he would depart from this world to the Father, having loved his own who were in the world, he loved them to the end. 2 During supper, the devil having already put into the heart of Judas Iscariot, Simon's son, to betray him, 3 Jesus, knowing that the Father had given all things into his hands, and that he came from God and was going to God, 4 arose from supper, and laid aside his outer garments. He took a towel and wrapped a towel around his waist. 5 Then he poured water into the basin, and began to wash the disciples' feet and to wipe them with the towel that was wrapped around him. 6 Then he came to Simon Peter. He said to him, "Lord, do you wash my feet?"
7 Jesus answered him, "You don't know what I am doing now, but you will understand later."
8 Peter said to him, "You will never wash my feet!"
Jesus answered him, "If I don't wash you, you have no part with me."
9 Simon Peter said to him, "Lord, not my feet only, but also my hands and my head!"
10 Jesus said to him, "Someone who has bathed only needs to have his feet washed, but is completely clean. You are clean, but not all of you." 11 For he knew him who would betray him; therefore he said, "You are not all clean." 12 So when he had washed their feet, put his outer garment back on, and sat down again, he said to them, "Do you know what I have done to you? 13 You call me, 'Teacher' and 'Lord.' You say so correctly, for so I am. 14 If I then, the Lord and the Teacher, have washed your feet, you also ought to wash one another's feet. 15 For I have given you an example, that you should also do as I have done to you.

1. Invite the Holy Spirit into this reading, asking the Author of Scripture to speak to you through His Word
2. Read today's passage as many times as you need, take your time
3. Write down (below) what the Lord is saying to you today
4. Live with this Word in your heart through the day

Friday, April 18, 2025
Friday of the Passion of the Lord (Good Friday)

First Reading: Isaiah 52: 13 – 53: 12

¹³ Behold, my servant will deal wisely.
He will be exalted and lifted up,
and will be very high.
¹⁴ Just as many were astonished at you—
his appearance was marred more than any man, and his form more than the sons of men—
¹⁵ so he will cleanse⁺ many nations.
Kings will shut their mouths at him;
for they will see that which had not been told them,
and they will understand that which they had not heard.
¹ Who has believed our message?
To whom has Yahweh's arm been revealed?
² For he grew up before him as a tender plant,
and as a root out of dry ground.
He has no good looks or majesty.
When we see him, there is no beauty that we should desire him.
³ He was despised
and rejected by men,
a man of suffering
and acquainted with disease.
He was despised as one from whom men hide their face;
and we didn't respect him.
⁴ Surely he has borne our sickness
and carried our suffering;
yet we considered him plagued,

struck by God, and afflicted.

5 But he was pierced for our transgressions.

He was crushed for our iniquities.

The punishment that brought our peace was on him;

and by his wounds we are healed.

6 All we like sheep have gone astray.

Everyone has turned to his own way;

and Yahweh has laid on him the iniquity of us all.

7 He was oppressed,

yet when he was afflicted he didn't open his mouth.

As a lamb that is led to the slaughter,

and as a sheep that before its shearers is silent,

so he didn't open his mouth.

8 He was taken away by oppression and judgment.

As for his generation,

who considered that he was cut off out of the land of the living

and stricken for the disobedience of my people?

9 They made his grave with the wicked,

and with a rich man in his death,

although he had done no violence,

nor was any deceit in his mouth.

10 Yet it pleased Yahweh to bruise him.

He has caused him to suffer.

When you make his soul an offering for sin,

he will see his offspring.

He will prolong his days

and Yahweh's pleasure will prosper in his hand.

11 After the suffering of his soul,

he will see the light‡ and be satisfied.

My righteous servant will justify many by the knowledge of himself;

and he will bear their iniquities.

12 Therefore I will give him a portion with the great.

He will divide the plunder with the strong,

because he poured out his soul to death

and was counted with the transgressors;

yet he bore the sins of many

and made intercession for the transgressors.

Responsorial Psalm: Psalms 31: 2, 6, 12-13, 15-16, 17

² Bow down your ear to me.
Deliver me speedily.
Be to me a strong rock,
a house of defense to save me.
⁶ I hate those who regard lying vanities,
but I trust in Yahweh.
¹² I am forgotten from their hearts like a dead man.
I am like broken pottery.
¹³ For I have heard the slander of many, terror on every side,
while they conspire together against me,
they plot to take away my life.
¹⁵ My times are in your hand.
Deliver me from the hand of my enemies, and from those who persecute me.
¹⁶ Make your face to shine on your servant.
Save me in your loving kindness.
¹⁷ Let me not be disappointed, Yahweh, for I have called on you.
Let the wicked be disappointed.
Let them be silent in Sheol.⁺

Second Reading: Hebrews 4: 14-16; 5: 7-9

¹⁴ Having then a great high priest who has passed through the heavens, Jesus, the Son of God, let's hold tightly to our confession. ¹⁵ For we don't have a high priest who can't be touched with the feeling of our infirmities, but one who has been in all points tempted like we are, yet without sin. ¹⁶ Let's therefore draw near with boldness to the throne of grace, that we may receive mercy and may find grace for help in time of need.
⁷ He, in the days of his flesh, having offered up prayers and petitions with strong crying and tears to him who was able to save him from death, and having been heard for his godly fear, ⁸ though he was a Son, yet learned obedience by the things which he suffered. ⁹ Having been made perfect, he became to all of those who obey him the author of eternal salvation

Gospel: John 18: 1 – 19: 42

¹ When Jesus had spoken these words, he went out with his disciples over the brook Kidron, where there was a garden, into which he and his disciples entered. ² Now Judas, who betrayed him, also knew the place, for Jesus often met there with his disciples. ³ Judas then, having taken a detachment of soldiers and officers from the chief priests and the Pharisees, came there with lanterns, torches, and weapons. ⁴ Jesus therefore, knowing all the things that were happening to him, went out and said to them, "Who are you looking for?"

5 They answered him, "Jesus of Nazareth."

Jesus said to them, "I am he."

Judas also, who betrayed him, was standing with them. 6 When therefore he said to them, "I am he," they went backward and fell to the ground.

7 Again therefore he asked them, "Who are you looking for?"

They said, "Jesus of Nazareth."

8 Jesus answered, "I told you that I am he. If therefore you seek me, let these go their way," 9 that the word might be fulfilled which he spoke, "Of those whom you have given me, I have lost none."*

10 Simon Peter therefore, having a sword, drew it, struck the high priest's servant, and cut off his right ear. The servant's name was Malchus. 11 Jesus therefore said to Peter, "Put the sword into its sheath. The cup which the Father has given me, shall I not surely drink it?"

12 So the detachment, the commanding officer, and the officers of the Jews seized Jesus and bound him, 13 and led him to Annas first, for he was father-in-law to Caiaphas, who was high priest that year. 14 Now it was Caiaphas who advised the Jews that it was expedient that one man should perish for the people.

15 Simon Peter followed Jesus, as did another disciple. Now that disciple was known to the high priest, and entered in with Jesus into the court of the high priest; 16 but Peter was standing at the door outside. So the other disciple, who was known to the high priest, went out and spoke to her who kept the door, and brought in Peter. 17 Then the maid who kept the door said to Peter, "Are you also one of this man's disciples?"

He said, "I am not."

18 Now the servants and the officers were standing there, having made a fire of coals, for it was cold. They were warming themselves. Peter was with them, standing and warming himself.

19 The high priest therefore asked Jesus about his disciples and about his teaching.

20 Jesus answered him, "I spoke openly to the world. I always taught in synagogues and in the temple, where the Jews always meet. I said nothing in secret. 21 Why do you ask me? Ask those who have heard me what I said to them. Behold, they know the things which I said."

22 When he had said this, one of the officers standing by slapped Jesus with his hand, saying, "Do you answer the high priest like that?"

23 Jesus answered him, "If I have spoken evil, testify of the evil; but if well, why do you beat me?"

24 Annas sent him bound to Caiaphas, the high priest.

25 Now Simon Peter was standing and warming himself. They said therefore to him, "You aren't also one of his disciples, are you?"

He denied it and said, "I am not."

26 One of the servants of the high priest, being a relative of him whose ear Peter had cut off, said, "Didn't I see you in the garden with him?"

27 Peter therefore denied it again, and immediately the rooster crowed.

28 They led Jesus therefore from Caiaphas into the Praetorium. It was early, and they themselves didn't enter into the Praetorium, that they might not be defiled, but might eat the Passover. 29 Pilate therefore went out to them and said, "What accusation do you bring against this man?"

30 They answered him, "If this man weren't an evildoer, we wouldn't have delivered him up to you."

31 Pilate therefore said to them, "Take him yourselves, and judge him according to your law."

Therefore the Jews said to him, "It is illegal for us to put anyone to death," 32 that the word of Jesus might be fulfilled, which he spoke, signifying by what kind of death he should die.

33 Pilate therefore entered again into the Praetorium, called Jesus, and said to him, "Are you the King of the Jews?"

34 Jesus answered him, "Do you say this by yourself, or did others tell you about me?"

35 Pilate answered, "I'm not a Jew, am I? Your own nation and the chief priests delivered you to me. What have you done?"

36 Jesus answered, "My Kingdom is not of this world. If my Kingdom were of this world, then my servants would fight, that I wouldn't be delivered to the Jews. But now my Kingdom is not from here."

37 Pilate therefore said to him, "Are you a king then?"

Jesus answered, "You say that I am a king. For this reason I have been born, and for this reason I have come into the world, that I should testify to the truth. Everyone who is of the truth listens to my voice."

38 Pilate said to him, "What is truth?"

When he had said this, he went out again to the Jews, and said to them, "I find no basis for a charge against him. 39 But you have a custom that I should release someone to you at the Passover. Therefore, do you want me to release to you the King of the Jews?"

40 Then they all shouted again, saying, "Not this man, but Barabbas!" Now Barabbas was a robber.

1 So Pilate then took Jesus and flogged him. 2 The soldiers twisted thorns into a crown and put it on his head, and dressed him in a purple garment. 3 They kept saying, "Hail, King of the Jews!" and they kept slapping him.

4 Then Pilate went out again, and said to them, "Behold, I bring him out to you, that you may know that I find no basis for a charge against him."

5 Jesus therefore came out, wearing the crown of thorns and the purple garment. Pilate said to them, "Behold, the man!"

6 When therefore the chief priests and the officers saw him, they shouted, saying, "Crucify! Crucify!"

Pilate said to them, "Take him yourselves and crucify him, for I find no basis for a charge against him."

7 The Jews answered him, "We have a law, and by our law he ought to die, because he made himself the Son of God."

8 When therefore Pilate heard this saying, he was more afraid. 9 He entered into the Praetorium again, and said to Jesus, "Where are you from?" But Jesus gave him no answer. 10 Pilate therefore said to him, "Aren't you speaking to me? Don't you know that I have power to release you and have power to crucify you?"

11 Jesus answered, "You would have no power at all against me, unless it were given to you from above. Therefore he who delivered me to you has greater sin."

12 At this, Pilate was seeking to release him, but the Jews cried out, saying, "If you release this man, you aren't Caesar's friend! Everyone who makes himself a king speaks against Caesar!"

13 When Pilate therefore heard these words, he brought Jesus out and sat down on the judgment seat at a place called "The Pavement", but in Hebrew, "Gabbatha." 14 Now it was the Preparation Day of the Passover, at about the sixth hour.[±] He said to the Jews, "Behold, your King!"

15 They cried out, "Away with him! Away with him! Crucify him!"

Pilate said to them, "Shall I crucify your King?"

The chief priests answered, "We have no king but Caesar!"

16 So then he delivered him to them to be crucified. So they took Jesus and led him away. 17 He went out, bearing his cross, to the place called "The Place of a Skull", which is called in Hebrew, "Golgotha", 18 where they crucified him, and with him two others, on either side one, and Jesus in the middle. 19 Pilate wrote a title also, and put it on the cross. There was written, "JESUS OF NAZARETH, THE KING OF THE JEWS." 20 Therefore many of the Jews read this title, for the place where Jesus was crucified was near the city; and it was written in Hebrew, in Latin, and in Greek. 21 The chief priests of the Jews therefore said to Pilate, "Don't write, 'The King of the Jews,' but, 'he said, "I am King of the Jews." ' "

22 Pilate answered, "What I have written, I have written."

23 Then the soldiers, when they had crucified Jesus, took his garments and made four parts, to every soldier a part; and also the tunic. Now the tunic was without seam, woven from the top throughout. 24 Then they said to one another, "Let's not tear it, but cast lots for it to decide whose it will be," that the Scripture might be fulfilled, which says,

"They parted my garments among them.
They cast lots for my clothing."[±]

Therefore the soldiers did these things.

25 But standing by Jesus' cross were his mother, his mother's sister, Mary the wife of Clopas, and Mary Magdalene. 26 Therefore when Jesus saw his mother, and the disciple whom he loved standing there, he said to his mother, "Woman, behold, your son!" 27 Then he said to the disciple, "Behold, your mother!" From that hour, the disciple took her to his own home.

28 After this, Jesus, seeing‡ that all things were now finished, that the Scripture might be fulfilled, said, "I am thirsty!" 29 Now a vessel full of vinegar was set there; so they put a sponge full of the vinegar on hyssop, and held it at his mouth. 30 When Jesus therefore had received the vinegar, he said, "It is finished!" Then he bowed his head and gave up his spirit.

31 Therefore the Jews, because it was the Preparation Day, so that the bodies wouldn't remain on the cross on the Sabbath (for that Sabbath was a special one), asked of Pilate that their legs might be broken and that they might be taken away. 32 Therefore the soldiers came and broke the legs of the first and of the other who was crucified with him; 33 but when they came to Jesus and saw that he was already dead, they didn't break his legs. 34 However, one of the soldiers pierced his side with a spear, and immediately blood and water came out. 35 He who has seen has testified, and his testimony is true. He knows that he tells the truth, that you may believe. 36 For these things happened that the Scripture might be fulfilled, "A bone of him will not be broken."* 37 Again another Scripture says, "They will look on him whom they pierced."*

38 After these things, Joseph of Arimathaea, being a disciple of Jesus, but secretly for fear of the Jews, asked of Pilate that he might take away Jesus' body. Pilate gave him permission. He came therefore and took away his body. 39 Nicodemus, who at first came to Jesus by night, also came bringing a mixture of myrrh and aloes, about a hundred Roman pounds.§ 40 So they took Jesus' body, and bound it in linen cloths with the spices, as the custom of the Jews is to bury. 41 Now in the place where he was crucified there was a garden. In the garden was a new tomb in which no man had ever yet been laid. 42 Then, because of the Jews' Preparation Day (for the tomb was near at hand), they laid Jesus there.

1. Invite the Holy Spirit into this reading, asking the Author of Scripture to speak to you through His Word
2. Read today's passage as many times as you need, take your time
3. Write down (below) what the Lord is saying to you today
4. Live with this Word in your heart through the day

Saturday, April 19, 2025
Holy Saturday

First Reading: Genesis 1: 1, 26-31a

[1] In the beginning, God[±] created the heavens and the earth.

[26] God said, "Let's make man in our image, after our likeness. Let them have dominion over the fish of the sea, and over the birds of the sky, and over the livestock, and over all the earth, and over every creeping thing that creeps on the earth." [27] God created man in his own image. In God's image he created him; male and female he created them. [28] God blessed them. God said to them, "Be fruitful, multiply, fill the earth, and subdue it. Have dominion over the fish of the sea, over the birds of the sky, and over every living thing that moves on the earth." [29] God said, "Behold,[‡] I have given you every herb yielding seed, which is on the surface of all the earth, and every tree, which bears fruit yielding seed. It will be your food. [30] To every animal of the earth, and to every bird of the sky, and to everything that creeps on the earth, in which there is life, I have given every green herb for food;" and it was so.

[31] God saw everything that he had made, and, behold, it was very good.

Responsorial Psalm: Psalms 104: 1-2, 5-6, 10, 12, 13-14, 24, 35

[1] Bless Yahweh, my soul.
Yahweh, my God, you are very great.
You are clothed with honor and majesty.
[2] He covers himself with light as with a garment.
He stretches out the heavens like a curtain.
[5] He laid the foundations of the earth,
that it should not be moved forever.
[6] You covered it with the deep as with a cloak.
The waters stood above the mountains.
[10] He sends springs into the valleys.
They run among the mountains.
[12] The birds of the sky nest by them.
They sing among the branches.
[13] He waters the mountains from his rooms.
The earth is filled with the fruit of your works.
[14] He causes the grass to grow for the livestock,
and plants for man to cultivate,
that he may produce food out of the earth:
[24] Yahweh, how many are your works!
In wisdom, you have made them all.
The earth is full of your riches.
[35] Let sinners be consumed out of the earth.
Let the wicked be no more.
Bless Yahweh, my soul.

Praise Yah!

Second Reading: Genesis 22: 1-2, 9, 10-13, 15-18

[1] After these things, God tested Abraham, and said to him, "Abraham!"
He said, "Here I am."
[2] He said, "Now take your son, your only son, Isaac, whom you love, and go into the land of Moriah. Offer him there as a burnt offering on one of the mountains which I will tell you of."
[9] They came to the place which God had told him of. Abraham built the altar there, and laid the wood in order, bound Isaac his son, and laid him on the altar, on the wood. [10] Abraham stretched out his hand, and took the knife to kill his son.
[11] Yahweh's angel called to him out of the sky, and said, "Abraham, Abraham!"
He said, "Here I am."
[12] He said, "Don't lay your hand on the boy or do anything to him. For now I know that you fear God, since you have not withheld your son, your only son, from me."
[13] Abraham lifted up his eyes, and looked, and saw that behind him was a ram caught in the thicket by his horns. Abraham went and took the ram, and offered him up for a burnt offering instead of his son.
[15] Yahweh's angel called to Abraham a second time out of the sky, [16] and said, " 'I have sworn by myself,' says Yahweh, 'because you have done this thing, and have not withheld your son, your only son, [17] that I will bless you greatly, and I will multiply your offspring greatly like the stars of the heavens, and like the sand which is on the seashore. Your offspring will possess the gate of his enemies. [18] All the nations of the earth will be blessed by your offspring, because you have obeyed my voice.' "

Responsorial Psalm: Psalms 16: 5, 8, 9-10, 11

[5] Yahweh assigned my portion and my cup.
You made my lot secure.
[8] I have set Yahweh always before me.
Because he is at my right hand, I shall not be moved.
[9] Therefore my heart is glad, and my tongue rejoices.
My body shall also dwell in safety.
[10] For you will not leave my soul in Sheol,[‡]
neither will you allow your holy one to see corruption.
[11] You will show me the path of life.
In your presence is fullness of joy.
In your right hand there are pleasures forever more.

Third Reading: Exodus 14: 15 – 15: 1

15 Yahweh said to Moses, "Why do you cry to me? Speak to the children of Israel, that they go forward. 16 Lift up your rod, and stretch out your hand over the sea and divide it. Then the children of Israel shall go into the middle of the sea on dry ground. 17 Behold, I myself will harden the hearts of the Egyptians, and they will go in after them. I will get myself honor over Pharaoh, and over all his armies, over his chariots, and over his horsemen. 18 The Egyptians shall know that I am Yahweh when I have gotten myself honor over Pharaoh, over his chariots, and over his horsemen." 19 The angel of God, who went before the camp of Israel, moved and went behind them; and the pillar of cloud moved from before them, and stood behind them. 20 It came between the camp of Egypt and the camp of Israel. There was the cloud and the darkness, yet it gave light by night. One didn't come near the other all night.

21 Moses stretched out his hand over the sea, and Yahweh caused the sea to go back by a strong east wind all night, and made the sea dry land, and the waters were divided. 22 The children of Israel went into the middle of the sea on the dry ground; and the waters were a wall to them on their right hand and on their left. 23 The Egyptians pursued, and went in after them into the middle of the sea: all of Pharaoh's horses, his chariots, and his horsemen. 24 In the morning watch, Yahweh looked out on the Egyptian army through the pillar of fire and of cloud, and confused the Egyptian army. 25 He took off their chariot wheels, and they drove them heavily; so that the Egyptians said, "Let's flee from the face of Israel, for Yahweh fights for them against the Egyptians!"

26 Yahweh said to Moses, "Stretch out your hand over the sea, that the waters may come again on the Egyptians, on their chariots, and on their horsemen." 27 Moses stretched out his hand over the sea, and the sea returned to its strength when the morning appeared; and the Egyptians fled against it. Yahweh overthrew the Egyptians in the middle of the sea. 28 The waters returned, and covered the chariots and the horsemen, even all Pharaoh's army that went in after them into the sea. There remained not so much as one of them. 29 But the children of Israel walked on dry land in the middle of the sea, and the waters were a wall to them on their right hand and on their left. 30 Thus Yahweh saved Israel that day out of the hand of the Egyptians; and Israel saw the Egyptians dead on the seashore. 31 Israel saw the great work which Yahweh did to the Egyptians, and the people feared Yahweh; and they believed in Yahweh and in his servant Moses.

1 Then Moses and the children of Israel sang this song to Yahweh, and said,
"I will sing to Yahweh, for he has triumphed gloriously.
He has thrown the horse and his rider into the sea.

Responsorial Psalm: Exodus 15: 1-6, 17-18

1 Then Moses and the children of Israel sang this song to Yahweh, and said,

"I will sing to Yahweh, for he has triumphed gloriously.
He has thrown the horse and his rider into the sea.
2 Yah is my strength and song.
He has become my salvation.
This is my God, and I will praise him;
my father's God, and I will exalt him.
3 Yahweh is a man of war.
Yahweh is his name.
4 He has cast Pharaoh's chariots and his army into the sea.
His chosen captains are sunk in the Red Sea.
5 The deeps cover them.
They went down into the depths like a stone.
6 Your right hand, Yahweh, is glorious in power.
Your right hand, Yahweh, dashes the enemy in pieces.
17 You will bring them in, and plant them in the mountain of your inheritance,
the place, Yahweh, which you have made for yourself to dwell in:
the sanctuary, Lord, which your hands have established.
18 Yahweh will reign forever and ever."

Fourth Reading: Isaiah 54: 5-14

5 For your Maker is your husband; Yahweh of Armies is his name.
The Holy One of Israel is your Redeemer.
He will be called the God of the whole earth.
6 For Yahweh has called you as a wife forsaken and grieved in spirit,
even a wife of youth, when she is cast off," says your God.
7 "For a small moment I have forsaken you,
but I will gather you with great mercies.
8 In overflowing wrath I hid my face from you for a moment,
but with everlasting loving kindness I will have mercy on you," says Yahweh your Redeemer.
9 "For this is like the waters of Noah to me;
for as I have sworn that the waters of Noah will no more go over the earth,
so I have sworn that I will not be angry with you, nor rebuke you.
10 For the mountains may depart,
and the hills be removed,
but my loving kindness will not depart from you,
and my covenant of peace will not be removed,"
says Yahweh who has mercy on you.
11 "You afflicted, tossed with storms, and not comforted,

behold, I will set your stones in beautiful colors,
and lay your foundations with sapphires.
¹² I will make your pinnacles of rubies,
your gates of sparkling jewels,
and all your walls of precious stones.
¹³ All your children will be taught by Yahweh,
and your children's peace will be great.
¹⁴ You will be established in righteousness.
You will be far from oppression,
for you will not be afraid,
and far from terror,
for it shall not come near you.

Responsorial Psalm: Psalms 30: 2, 4, 5-6, 11-12

² Yahweh my God, I cried to you,
and you have healed me.
⁴ Sing praise to Yahweh, you saints of his.
Give thanks to his holy name.
⁵ For his anger is but for a moment.
His favor is for a lifetime.
Weeping may stay for the night,
but joy comes in the morning.
⁶ As for me, I said in my prosperity,
"I shall never be moved."
¹¹ You have turned my mourning into dancing for me.
You have removed my sackcloth, and clothed me with gladness,
¹² to the end that my heart may sing praise to you, and not be silent.
Yahweh my God, I will give thanks to you forever!

Fifth Reading: Isaiah 55: 1-11

¹ "Hey! Come, everyone who thirsts, to the waters!
Come, he who has no money, buy, and eat!
Yes, come, buy wine and milk without money and without price.
² Why do you spend money for that which is not bread,
and your labor for that which doesn't satisfy?
Listen diligently to me, and eat that which is good,
and let your soul delight itself in richness.
³ Turn your ear, and come to me.

Hear, and your soul will live.

I will make an everlasting covenant with you, even the sure mercies of David.

4 Behold, I have given him for a witness to the peoples,

a leader and commander to the peoples.

5 Behold, you shall call a nation that you don't know;

and a nation that didn't know you shall run to you,

because of Yahweh your God,

and for the Holy One of Israel;

for he has glorified you."

6 Seek Yahweh while he may be found.

Call on him while he is near.

7 Let the wicked forsake his way,

and the unrighteous man his thoughts.

Let him return to Yahweh, and he will have mercy on him,

to our God, for he will freely pardon.

8 "For my thoughts are not your thoughts,

and your ways are not my ways," says Yahweh.

9 "For as the heavens are higher than the earth,

so are my ways higher than your ways,

and my thoughts than your thoughts.

10 For as the rain comes down and the snow from the sky,

and doesn't return there, but waters the earth,

and makes it grow and bud,

and gives seed to the sower and bread to the eater;

11 so is my word that goes out of my mouth:

it will not return to me void,

but it will accomplish that which I please,

and it will prosper in the thing I sent it to do.

Responsorial Psalm: Isaiah 12: 2-3, 4, 5-6

2 Behold, God is my salvation. I will trust, and will not be afraid; for Yah, Yahweh, is my strength and song; and he has become my salvation." 3 Therefore with joy you will draw water out of the wells of salvation.

4 In that day you will say, "Give thanks to Yahweh! Call on his name! Declare his doings among the peoples! Proclaim that his name is exalted!

5 Sing to Yahweh, for he has done excellent things! Let this be known in all the earth! 6 Cry aloud and shout, you inhabitant of Zion, for the Holy One of Israel is great among you!"

Sixth Reading: Baruch 3: 9-15, 32 – 4: 4

9 Hear, O Israel, the commandments of life! Give ear to understand wisdom! 10 How is it, O Israel, that you are in your enemies' land, that you have become old in a strange country, that you are defiled with the dead, 11 that you are counted with those who are in Hades? 12 You have forsaken the fountain of wisdom. 13 If you had walked in the way of God, you would have dwelled in peace forever. 14 Learn where there is wisdom, where there is strength, and where there is understanding, that you may also know where there is length of days and life, where there is the light of the eyes and peace. 15 Who has found out her place? Who has come into her treasuries?

32 But he that knows all things knows her, he found her out with his understanding. He who prepared the earth for all time has filled it with four-footed beasts. 33 It is he who sends forth the light, and it goes. He called it, and it obeyed him with fear. 34 The stars shone in their watches, and were glad. When he called them, they said, "Here we are." They shone with gladness to him who made them. 35 This is our God. No other can be compared to him. 36 He has found out all the way of knowledge, and has given it to Jacob his servant and to Israel who is loved by him. 37 Afterward she appeared upon earth, and lived with men.

1 This is the book of God's commandments and the law that endures forever. All those who hold it fast will live, but those who leave it will die. 2 Turn, O Jacob, and take hold of it. Walk toward the shining of its light. 3 Don't give your glory to another, nor the things that are to your advantage to a foreign nation. 4 O Israel, we are happy; for the things that are pleasing to God are made known to us.

Responsorial Psalm: Psalms 19: 8, 9, 10, 11

8 Yahweh's precepts are right, rejoicing the heart.
Yahweh's commandment is pure, enlightening the eyes.
9 The fear of Yahweh is clean, enduring forever.
Yahweh's ordinances are true, and righteous altogether.
10 They are more to be desired than gold, yes, than much fine gold,
sweeter also than honey and the extract of the honeycomb.
11 Moreover your servant is warned by them.
In keeping them there is great reward.

Seventh Reading: Ezekiel 36: 16-17a, 18-28

16 Moreover Yahweh's word came to me, saying, 17 "Son of man, when the house of Israel lived in their own land, they defiled it by their ways and by their deeds.
18 Therefore I poured out my wrath on them for the blood which they had poured out on the land, and because they had defiled it with their idols. 19 I scattered them among the nations, and they were dispersed through the countries. I judged them according to their

way and according to their deeds. ²⁰ When they came to the nations where they went, they profaned my holy name, in that men said of them, 'These are Yahweh's people, and have left his land.' ²¹ But I had respect for my holy name, which the house of Israel had profaned among the nations where they went.

²² "Therefore tell the house of Israel, 'The Lord Yahweh says: "I don't do this for your sake, house of Israel, but for my holy name, which you have profaned among the nations where you went. ²³ I will sanctify my great name, which has been profaned among the nations, which you have profaned among them. Then the nations will know that I am Yahweh," says the Lord Yahweh, "when I am proven holy in you before their eyes.

²⁴ " ' "For I will take you from among the nations and gather you out of all the countries, and will bring you into your own land. ²⁵ I will sprinkle clean water on you, and you will be clean. I will cleanse you from all your filthiness and from all your idols. ²⁶ I will also give you a new heart, and I will put a new spirit within you. I will take away the stony heart out of your flesh, and I will give you a heart of flesh. ²⁷ I will put my Spirit within you, and cause you to walk in my statutes. You will keep my ordinances and do them. ²⁸ You will dwell in the land that I gave to your fathers. You will be my people, and I will be your God.

Responsorial Psalm: Psalms 42: 3, 5; 43: 3, 4

³ My tears have been my food day and night,
while they continually ask me, "Where is your God?"
⁵ Why are you in despair, my soul?
Why are you disturbed within me?
Hope in God!
For I shall still praise him for the saving help of his presence.
³ Oh, send out your light and your truth.
Let them lead me.
Let them bring me to your holy hill,
to your tents.
⁴ Then I will go to the altar of God,
to God, my exceeding joy.
I will praise you on the harp, God, my God.

Epistle Reading: Romans 6: 3-11

³ Or don't you know that all of us who were baptized into Christ Jesus were baptized into his death? ⁴ We were buried therefore with him through baptism into death, that just as Christ was raised from the dead through the glory of the Father, so we also might walk in newness of life.

5 For if we have become united with him in the likeness of his death, we will also be part of his resurrection; 6 knowing this, that our old man was crucified with him, that the body of sin might be done away with, so that we would no longer be in bondage to sin. 7 For he who has died has been freed from sin. 8 But if we died with Christ, we believe that we will also live with him, 9 knowing that Christ, being raised from the dead, dies no more. Death no longer has dominion over him! 10 For the death that he died, he died to sin one time; but the life that he lives, he lives to God. 11 Thus consider yourselves also to be dead to sin, but alive to God in Christ Jesus our Lord.

Responsorial Psalm: Psalms 118: 1-2, 16-17, 22-23

1 Give thanks to Yahweh, for he is good,
for his loving kindness endures forever.
2 Let Israel now say
that his loving kindness endures forever.
16 The right hand of Yahweh is exalted!
The right hand of Yahweh does valiantly!"
17 I will not die, but live,
and declare Yah's works.
22 The stone which the builders rejected
has become the cornerstone.‡
23 This is Yahweh's doing.
It is marvelous in our eyes.

Gospel: Luke 24: 1-12

1 But on the first day of the week, at early dawn, they and some others came to the tomb, bringing the spices which they had prepared. 2 They found the stone rolled away from the tomb. 3 They entered in, and didn't find the Lord Jesus' body. 4 While they were greatly perplexed about this, behold, two men stood by them in dazzling clothing. 5 Becoming terrified, they bowed their faces down to the earth.
The men said to them, "Why do you seek the living among the dead? 6 He isn't here, but is risen. Remember what he told you when he was still in Galilee, 7 saying that the Son of Man must be delivered up into the hands of sinful men and be crucified, and the third day rise again?"
8 They remembered his words, 9 returned from the tomb, and told all these things to the eleven and to all the rest. 10 Now they were Mary Magdalene, Joanna, and Mary the mother of James. The other women with them told these things to the apostles. 11 These words seemed to them to be nonsense, and they didn't believe them. 12 But Peter got up and ran

to the tomb. Stooping and looking in, he saw the strips of linen lying by themselves, and he departed to his home, wondering what had happened.

1. Invite the Holy Spirit into this reading, asking the Author of Scripture to speak to you through His Word
2. Read today's passage as many times as you need, take your time
3. Write down (below) what the Lord is saying to you today
4. Live with this Word in your heart through the day

_____

_____

Sunday, April 20, 2025
EASTER SUNDAY OF THE RESURRECTION OF THE LORD

First Reading: Acts 10: 34a, 37-43

34a Peter opened his mouth and said,

37 you yourselves know what happened, which was proclaimed throughout all Judea, beginning from Galilee, after the baptism which John preached; 38 how God anointed Jesus of Nazareth with the Holy Spirit and with power, who went about doing good and healing all who were oppressed by the devil, for God was with him. 39 We are witnesses of everything he did both in the country of the Jews and in Jerusalem; whom they also‡ killed, hanging him on a tree. 40 God raised him up the third day and gave him to be revealed, 41 not to all the people, but to witnesses who were chosen before by God, to us, who ate and drank with him after he rose from the dead. 42 He commanded us to preach to the people and to testify that this is he who is appointed by God as the Judge of the living and the dead. 43 All the prophets testify about him, that through his name everyone who believes in him will receive remission of sins."

Responsorial Psalm: Psalms 118: 1-2, 16-17, 22-23

1 Give thanks to Yahweh, for he is good,
for his loving kindness endures forever.
2 Let Israel now say
that his loving kindness endures forever.
16 The right hand of Yahweh is exalted!
The right hand of Yahweh does valiantly!"

17 I will not die, but live,
and declare Yah's works.
22 The stone which the builders rejected
has become the cornerstone.⁺
23 This is Yahweh's doing.
It is marvelous in our eyes.

Second Reading: Colossians 3: 1-4

1 If then you were raised together with Christ, seek the things that are above, where Christ is, seated on the right hand of God. 2 Set your mind on the things that are above, not on the things that are on the earth. 3 For you died, and your life is hidden with Christ in God. 4 When Christ, our life, is revealed, then you will also be revealed with him in glory.

Gospel: John 20: 1-9

1 Now on the first day of the week, Mary Magdalene went early, while it was still dark, to the tomb, and saw that the stone had been taken away from the tomb. 2 Therefore she ran and came to Simon Peter and to the other disciple whom Jesus loved, and said to them, "They have taken away the Lord out of the tomb, and we don't know where they have laid him!"
3 Therefore Peter and the other disciple went out, and they went toward the tomb. 4 They both ran together. The other disciple outran Peter and came to the tomb first. 5 Stooping and looking in, he saw the linen cloths lying there; yet he didn't enter in. 6 Then Simon Peter came, following him, and entered into the tomb. He saw the linen cloths lying, 7 and the cloth that had been on his head, not lying with the linen cloths, but rolled up in a place by itself. 8 So then the other disciple who came first to the tomb also entered in, and he saw and believed. 9 For as yet they didn't know the Scripture, that he must rise from the dead.

1. Invite the Holy Spirit into this reading, asking the Author of Scripture to speak to you through His Word
2. Read today's passage as many times as you need, take your time
3. Write down (below) what the Lord is saying to you today
4. Live with this Word in your heart through the day

_____

_____

Easter Monday

First Reading: Acts 2: 14, 22-33

14 But Peter, standing up with the eleven, lifted up his voice and spoke out to them, "You men of Judea and all you who dwell at Jerusalem, let this be known to you, and listen to my words.

22 "Men of Israel, hear these words! Jesus of Nazareth, a man approved by God to you by mighty works and wonders and signs which God did by him among you, even as you yourselves know, 23 him, being delivered up by the determined counsel and foreknowledge of God, you have taken by the hand of lawless men, crucified and killed; 24 whom God raised up, having freed him from the agony of death, because it was not possible that he should be held by it. 25 For David says concerning him,

'I saw the Lord always before my face,

for he is on my right hand, that I should not be moved.

26 Therefore my heart was glad, and my tongue rejoiced.

Moreover my flesh also will dwell in hope,

27 because you will not leave my soul in Hades,‡

neither will you allow your Holy One to see decay.

28 You made known to me the ways of life.

You will make me full of gladness with your presence.'*

29 "Brothers, I may tell you freely of the patriarch David, that he both died and was buried, and his tomb is with us to this day. 30 Therefore, being a prophet, and knowing that God had sworn with an oath to him that of the fruit of his body, according to the flesh, he would raise up the Christ§ to sit on his throne, 31 he foreseeing this, spoke about the resurrection of the Christ, that his soul wasn't left in Hades,‡ and his flesh didn't see decay. 32 This Jesus God raised up, to which we all are witnesses. 33 Being therefore exalted by the right hand of God, and having received from the Father the promise of the Holy Spirit, he has poured out this which you now see and hear.

Responsorial Psalm: Psalms 16: 1-2a and 5, 7-8, 9-10, 11

1 Preserve me, God, for I take refuge in you.

2a My soul, you have said to Yahweh,

5 Yahweh assigned my portion and my cup.

You made my lot secure.

7 I will bless Yahweh, who has given me counsel.

Yes, my heart instructs me in the night seasons.

8 I have set Yahweh always before me.

Because he is at my right hand, I shall not be moved.

9 Therefore my heart is glad, and my tongue rejoices.

My body shall also dwell in safety.

10 For you will not leave my soul in Sheol,[‡]

neither will you allow your holy one to see corruption.

11 You will show me the path of life.

In your presence is fullness of joy.

In your right hand there are pleasures forever more.

Gospel: Matthew 28: 8-15

8 They departed quickly from the tomb with fear and great joy, and ran to bring his disciples word. 9 As they went to tell his disciples, behold, Jesus met them, saying, "Rejoice!"
They came and took hold of his feet, and worshiped him.
10 Then Jesus said to them, "Don't be afraid. Go tell my brothers [‡] that they should go into Galilee, and there they will see me."
11 Now while they were going, behold, some of the guards came into the city and told the chief priests all the things that had happened. 12 When they were assembled with the elders and had taken counsel, they gave a large amount of silver to the soldiers, 13 saying, "Say that his disciples came by night and stole him away while we slept. 14 If this comes to the governor's ears, we will persuade him and make you free of worry." 15 So they took the money and did as they were told. This saying was spread abroad among the Jews, and continues until today.

1. Invite the Holy Spirit into this reading, asking the Author of Scripture to speak to you through His Word
2. Read today's passage as many times as you need, take your time
3. Write down (below) what the Lord is saying to you today
4. Live with this Word in your heart through the day

_____

_____

Sunday, April 27, 2025
SECOND SUNDAY OF EASTER
SUNDAY OF DIVINE MERCY

First Reading: Acts 5: 12-16

¹² By the hands of the apostles many signs and wonders were done among the people. They were all with one accord in Solomon's porch. ¹³ None of the rest dared to join them; however, the people honored them. ¹⁴ More believers were added to the Lord, multitudes of both men and women. ¹⁵ They even carried out the sick into the streets and laid them on cots and mattresses, so that as Peter came by, at least his shadow might overshadow some of them. ¹⁶ The multitude also came together from the cities around Jerusalem, bringing sick people and those who were tormented by unclean spirits; and they were all healed.

Responsorial Psalm: Psalms 118: 2-4, 13-15, 22-24

² Let Israel now say
that his loving kindness endures forever.
³ Let the house of Aaron now say
that his loving kindness endures forever.
⁴ Now let those who fear Yahweh say
that his loving kindness endures forever.
¹³ You pushed me back hard, to make me fall,
but Yahweh helped me.
¹⁴ Yah is my strength and song.
He has become my salvation.
¹⁵ The voice of rejoicing and salvation is in the tents of the righteous.
"The right hand of Yahweh does valiantly.
²² The stone which the builders rejected
has become the cornerstone.ᵗ
²³ This is Yahweh's doing.
It is marvelous in our eyes.
²⁴ This is the day that Yahweh has made.
We will rejoice and be glad in it!

Second Reading: Revelation 1: 9-11a, 12-13, 17-19

⁹ I John, your brother and partner with you in the oppression, Kingdom, and perseverance in Christ Jesus, was on the isle that is called Patmos because of God's Word and the testimony of Jesus Christ. ¹⁰ I was in the Spirit on the Lord's day, and I heard behind me a loud voice, like a trumpet ¹¹ᵃ saying,§ "What you see, write in a book and send to the seven assemblies
¹² I turned to see the voice that spoke with me. Having turned, I saw seven golden lamp stands. ¹³ And among the lamp stands was one like a son of man,* clothed with a robe reaching down to his feet, and with a golden sash around his chest.

17 When I saw him, I fell at his feet like a dead man.

He laid his right hand on me, saying, "Don't be afraid. I am the first and the last, 18 and the Living one. I was dead, and behold, I am alive forever and ever. Amen. I have the keys of Death and of Hades.‡ 19 Write therefore the things which you have seen, and the things which are, and the things which will happen hereafter.

Gospel: John 20:19-31

19 When therefore it was evening on that day, the first day of the week, and when the doors were locked where the disciples were assembled, for fear of the Jews, Jesus came and stood in the middle and said to them, "Peace be to you."

20 When he had said this, he showed them his hands and his side. The disciples therefore were glad when they saw the Lord. 21 Jesus therefore said to them again, "Peace be to you. As the Father has sent me, even so I send you." 22 When he had said this, he breathed on them, and said to them, "Receive the Holy Spirit! 23 If you forgive anyone's sins, they have been forgiven them. If you retain anyone's sins, they have been retained."

24 But Thomas, one of the twelve, called Didymus,§ wasn't with them when Jesus came. 25 The other disciples therefore said to him, "We have seen the Lord!"

But he said to them, "Unless I see in his hands the print of the nails, put my finger into the print of the nails, and put my hand into his side, I will not believe."

26 After eight days, again his disciples were inside and Thomas was with them. Jesus came, the doors being locked, and stood in the middle, and said, "Peace be to you." 27 Then he said to Thomas, "Reach here your finger, and see my hands. Reach here your hand, and put it into my side. Don't be unbelieving, but believing."

28 Thomas answered him, "My Lord and my God!"

29 Jesus said to him, "Because you have seen me,‡ you have believed. Blessed are those who have not seen and have believed."

30 Therefore Jesus did many other signs in the presence of his disciples, which are not written in this book; 31 but these are written that you may believe that Jesus is the Christ, the Son of God, and that believing you may have life in his name.

1. Invite the Holy Spirit into this reading, asking the Author of Scripture to speak to you through His Word
2. Read today's passage as many times as you need, take your time
3. Write down (below) what the Lord is saying to you today
4. Live with this Word in your heart through the day

_____

_____

Sunday, May 4, 2025
THIRD SUNDAY OF EASTER

First Reading: Acts 5: 27-32, 40b-41

27 When they had brought them, they set them before the council. The high priest questioned them, 28 saying, "Didn't we strictly command you not to teach in this name? Behold, you have filled Jerusalem with your teaching, and intend to bring this man's blood on us."

29 But Peter and the apostles answered, "We must obey God rather than men. 30 The God of our fathers raised up Jesus, whom you killed, hanging him on a tree. 31 God exalted him with his right hand to be a Prince and a Savior, to give repentance to Israel, and remission of sins. 32 We are his witnesses of these things; and so also is the Holy Spirit, whom God has given to those who obey him."

40b Summoning the apostles, they beat them and commanded them not to speak in the name of Jesus, and let them go. 41 They therefore departed from the presence of the council, rejoicing that they were counted worthy to suffer dishonor for Jesus' name.

Responsorial Psalm: Psalms 30: 2 and 4, 5-6, 11-12

2 Yahweh my God, I cried to you,
and you have healed me.
4 Sing praise to Yahweh, you saints of his.
Give thanks to his holy name.
5 For his anger is but for a moment.
His favor is for a lifetime.
Weeping may stay for the night,
but joy comes in the morning.
6 As for me, I said in my prosperity,
"I shall never be moved."
11 You have turned my mourning into dancing for me.
You have removed my sackcloth, and clothed me with gladness,
12 to the end that my heart may sing praise to you, and not be silent.
Yahweh my God, I will give thanks to you forever!

Second Reading: Revelation 5: 11-14

11 I looked, and I heard something like a voice of many angels around the throne, the living creatures, and the elders. The number of them was ten thousands of ten thousands, and

thousands of thousands, [12] saying with a loud voice, "Worthy is the Lamb who has been killed to receive the power, wealth, wisdom, strength, honor, glory, and blessing!"

[13] I heard every created thing which is in heaven, on the earth, under the earth, on the sea, and everything in them, saying, "To him who sits on the throne and to the Lamb be the blessing, the honor, the glory, and the dominion, forever and ever! Amen!"[‡]

[14] The four living creatures said, "Amen!" Then the[‡] elders fell down and worshiped.

Gospel: John 21: 1-19

[1] After these things, Jesus revealed himself again to the disciples at the sea of Tiberias. He revealed himself this way. [2] Simon Peter, Thomas called Didymus,[‡] Nathanael of Cana in Galilee, and the sons of Zebedee, and two others of his disciples were together. [3] Simon Peter said to them, "I'm going fishing."

They told him, "We are also coming with you." They immediately went out and entered into the boat. That night, they caught nothing. [4] But when day had already come, Jesus stood on the beach; yet the disciples didn't know that it was Jesus. [5] Jesus therefore said to them, "Children, have you anything to eat?"

They answered him, "No."

[6] He said to them, "Cast the net on the right side of the boat, and you will find some."

They cast it therefore, and now they weren't able to draw it in for the multitude of fish. [7] That disciple therefore whom Jesus loved said to Peter, "It's the Lord!"

So when Simon Peter heard that it was the Lord, he wrapped his coat around himself (for he was naked), and threw himself into the sea. [8] But the other disciples came in the little boat (for they were not far from the land, but about two hundred cubits[‡] away), dragging the net full of fish. [9] So when they got out on the land, they saw a fire of coals there, with fish and bread laid on it. [10] Jesus said to them, "Bring some of the fish which you have just caught."

[11] Simon Peter went up, and drew the net to land, full of one hundred fifty-three great fish. Even though there were so many, the net wasn't torn.

[12] Jesus said to them, "Come and eat breakfast!"

None of the disciples dared inquire of him, "Who are you?" knowing that it was the Lord.

[13] Then Jesus came and took the bread, gave it to them, and the fish likewise. [14] This is now the third time that Jesus was revealed to his disciples after he had risen from the dead. [15] So when they had eaten their breakfast, Jesus said to Simon Peter, "Simon, son of Jonah, do you love me more than these?"

He said to him, "Yes, Lord; you know that I have affection for you."

He said to him, "Feed my lambs." [16] He said to him again a second time, "Simon, son of Jonah, do you love me?"

He said to him, "Yes, Lord; you know that I have affection for you."

He said to him, "Tend my sheep." ¹⁷ He said to him the third time, "Simon, son of Jonah, do you have affection for me?"

Peter was grieved because he asked him the third time, "Do you have affection for me?" He said to him, "Lord, you know everything. You know that I have affection for you."

Jesus said to him, "Feed my sheep. ¹⁸ Most certainly I tell you, when you were young, you dressed yourself and walked where you wanted to. But when you are old, you will stretch out your hands, and another will dress you and carry you where you don't want to go."

¹⁹ Now he said this, signifying by what kind of death he would glorify God. When he had said this, he said to him, "Follow me."

1. Invite the Holy Spirit into this reading, asking the Author of Scripture to speak to you through His Word
2. Read today's passage as many times as you need, take your time
3. Write down (below) what the Lord is saying to you today
4. Live with this Word in your heart through the day

Sunday, May 11, 2025
FOURTH SUNDAY OF EASTER

First Reading: Acts 13: 14, 43-52

¹⁴ But they, passing on from Perga, came to Antioch of Pisidia. They went into the synagogue on the Sabbath day and sat down.

⁴³ Now when the synagogue broke up, many of the Jews and of the devout proselytes followed Paul and Barnabas; who, speaking to them, urged them to continue in the grace of God.

⁴⁴ The next Sabbath, almost the whole city was gathered together to hear the word of God. ⁴⁵ But when the Jews saw the multitudes, they were filled with jealousy, and contradicted the things which were spoken by Paul, and blasphemed.

⁴⁶ Paul and Barnabas spoke out boldly, and said, "It was necessary that God's word should be spoken to you first. Since indeed you thrust it from yourselves, and judge yourselves unworthy of eternal life, behold, we turn to the Gentiles. ⁴⁷ For so has the Lord commanded us, saying,

'I have set you as a light for the Gentiles,

that you should bring salvation to the uttermost parts of the earth.' " *

⁴⁸ As the Gentiles heard this, they were glad and glorified the word of God. As many as were appointed to eternal life believed. ⁴⁹ The Lord's word was spread abroad throughout all the region. ⁵⁰ But the Jews stirred up the devout and prominent women and the chief men of the city, and stirred up a persecution against Paul and Barnabas, and threw them out of their borders. ⁵¹ But they shook off the dust of their feet against them, and came to Iconium. ⁵² The disciples were filled with joy and with the Holy Spirit.

Responsorial Psalm: Psalms 100: 1-2, 3, 5

¹ Shout for joy to Yahweh, all you lands!
² Serve Yahweh with gladness.
Come before his presence with singing.
³ Know that Yahweh, he is God.
It is he who has made us, and we are his.
We are his people, and the sheep of his pasture.
⁵ For Yahweh is good.
His loving kindness endures forever,
his faithfulness to all generations.

Second Reading: Revelation 7: 9, 14b-17

⁹ After these things I looked, and behold, a great multitude which no man could count, out of every nation and of all tribes, peoples, and languages, standing before the throne and before the Lamb, dressed in white robes, with palm branches in their hands.
¹⁴ᵇ He said to me, "These are those who came out of the great suffering.‡ They washed their robes and made them white in the Lamb's blood. ¹⁵ Therefore they are before the throne of God, and they serve him day and night in his temple. He who sits on the throne will spread his tabernacle over them. ¹⁶ They will never be hungry or thirsty any more. The sun won't beat on them, nor any heat; ¹⁷ for the Lamb who is in the middle of the throne shepherds them and leads them to springs of life-giving waters. And God will wipe away every tear from their eyes."

Gospel: John 10: 27-30

²⁷ My sheep hear my voice, and I know them, and they follow me. ²⁸ I give eternal life to them. They will never perish, and no one will snatch them out of my hand. ²⁹ My Father who has given them to me is greater than all. No one is able to snatch them out of my Father's hand. ³⁰ I and the Father are one."

1. Invite the Holy Spirit into this reading, asking the Author of Scripture to speak to you through His Word
2. Read today's passage as many times as you need, take your time
3. Write down (below) what the Lord is saying to you today
4. Live with this Word in your heart through the day

Sunday, May 18, 2025
FIFTH SUNDAY OF EASTER

First Reading: Acts 14: 21-27

21 When they had preached the Good News to that city and had made many disciples, they returned to Lystra, Iconium, and Antioch, 22 strengthening the souls of the disciples, exhorting them to continue in the faith, and that through many afflictions we must enter into God's Kingdom. 23 When they had appointed elders for them in every assembly, and had prayed with fasting, they commended them to the Lord on whom they had believed. 24 They passed through Pisidia and came to Pamphylia. 25 When they had spoken the word in Perga, they went down to Attalia. 26 From there they sailed to Antioch, from where they had been committed to the grace of God for the work which they had fulfilled. 27 When they had arrived and had gathered the assembly together, they reported all the things that God had done with them, and that he had opened a door of faith to the nations.

Responsorial Psalm: Psalms 145: 8-13

8 Yahweh is gracious, merciful,
slow to anger, and of great loving kindness.
9 Yahweh is good to all.
His tender mercies are over all his works.
10 All your works will give thanks to you, Yahweh.
Your saints will extol you.
11 They will speak of the glory of your kingdom,
and talk about your power,
12 to make known to the sons of men his mighty acts,
the glory of the majesty of his kingdom.
13 Your kingdom is an everlasting kingdom.

Your dominion endures throughout all generations.
Yahweh is faithful in all his words,
and loving in all his deeds.

Second Reading: Revelation 21: 1-5a

[1] I saw a new heaven and a new earth, for the first heaven and the first earth have passed away, and the sea is no more. [2] I saw the holy city, New Jerusalem, coming down out of heaven from God, prepared like a bride adorned for her husband. [3] I heard a loud voice out of heaven saying, "Behold, God's dwelling is with people; and he will dwell with them, and they will be his people, and God himself will be with them as their God. [4] He will wipe away every tear from their eyes. Death will be no more; neither will there be mourning, nor crying, nor pain any more. The first things have passed away."
[5a] He who sits on the throne said, "Behold, I am making all things new."

Gospel: John 13: 31-33a, 34-35

[31] When he had gone out, Jesus said, "Now the Son of Man has been glorified, and God has been glorified in him. [32] If God has been glorified in him, God will also glorify him in himself, and he will glorify him immediately. [33a] Little children, I will be with you a little while longer.
[34] A new commandment I give to you, that you love one another. Just as I have loved you, you also love one another. [35] By this everyone will know that you are my disciples, if you have love for one another."

1. Invite the Holy Spirit into this reading, asking the Author of Scripture to speak to you through His Word
2. Read today's passage as many times as you need, take your time
3. Write down (below) what the Lord is saying to you today
4. Live with this Word in your heart through the day

_____

_____

Sunday, May 25, 2025
SIXTH SUNDAY OF EASTER

First Reading: Acts 15: 1-2, 22-29

¹ Some men came down from Judea and taught the brothers,⁑ "Unless you are circumcised after the custom of Moses, you can't be saved." ² Therefore when Paul and Barnabas had no small discord and discussion with them, they appointed Paul, Barnabas, and some others of them to go up to Jerusalem to the apostles and elders about this question.

²² Then it seemed good to the apostles and the elders, with the whole assembly, to choose men out of their company, and send them to Antioch with Paul and Barnabas: Judas called Barsabbas, and Silas, chief men among the brothers.§ ²³ They wrote these things by their hand:

"The apostles, the elders, and the brothers, to the brothers who are of the Gentiles in Antioch, Syria, and Cilicia: greetings. ²⁴ Because we have heard that some who went out from us have troubled you with words, unsettling your souls, saying, 'You must be circumcised and keep the law,' to whom we gave no commandment; ²⁵ it seemed good to us, having come to one accord, to choose out men and send them to you with our beloved Barnabas and Paul, ²⁶ men who have risked their lives for the name of our Lord Jesus Christ. ²⁷ We have sent therefore Judas and Silas, who themselves will also tell you the same things by word of mouth. ²⁸ For it seemed good to the Holy Spirit, and to us, to lay no greater burden on you than these necessary things: ²⁹ that you abstain from things sacrificed to idols, from blood, from things strangled, and from sexual immorality, from which if you keep yourselves, it will be well with you. Farewell."

Responsorial Psalm: Psalms 67: 2-3, 5, 6

² That your way may be known on earth,
and your salvation among all nations,
³ let the peoples praise you, God.
Let all the peoples praise you.
⁵ Let the peoples praise you, God.
Let all the peoples praise you.
⁶ The earth has yielded its increase.
God, even our own God, will bless us.

Second Reading: Revelation 21: 10-14, 22-23

¹⁰ He carried me away in the Spirit to a great and high mountain, and showed me the holy city, Jerusalem, coming down out of heaven from God, ¹¹ having the glory of God. Her light was like a most precious stone, like a jasper stone, clear as crystal; ¹² having a great and high wall with twelve gates, and at the gates twelve angels, and names written on them, which are the names of the twelve tribes of the children of Israel. ¹³ On the east were three gates, and on the north three gates, and on the south three gates, and on the west three

gates. ¹⁴ The wall of the city had twelve foundations, and on them twelve names of the twelve Apostles of the Lamb.

²² I saw no temple in it, for the Lord God the Almighty and the Lamb are its temple. ²³ The city has no need for the sun or moon to shine, for the very glory of God illuminated it and its lamp is the Lamb.

Gospel: John 14: 23-29

²³ Jesus answered him, "If a man loves me, he will keep my word. My Father will love him, and we will come to him and make our home with him. ²⁴ He who doesn't love me doesn't keep my words. The word which you hear isn't mine, but the Father's who sent me. ²⁵ "I have said these things to you while still living with you. ²⁶ But the Counselor, the Holy Spirit, whom the Father will send in my name, will teach you all things, and will remind you of all that I said to you. ²⁷ Peace I leave with you. My peace I give to you; not as the world gives, I give to you. Don't let your heart be troubled, neither let it be fearful. ²⁸ You heard how I told you, 'I am going away, and I will come back to you.' If you loved me, you would have rejoiced because I said 'I am going to my Father;' for the Father is greater than I. ²⁹ Now I have told you before it happens so that when it happens, you may believe.

1. Invite the Holy Spirit into this reading, asking the Author of Scripture to speak to you through His Word
2. Read today's passage as many times as you need, take your time
3. Write down (below) what the Lord is saying to you today
4. Live with this Word in your heart through the day

_____

_____

Thursday, May 29, 2025
Saint Paul VI, Pope

First Reading: Acts 18: 1-8

¹ After these things Paul departed from Athens and came to Corinth. ² He found a certain Jew named Aquila, a man of Pontus by race, who had recently come from Italy with his wife Priscilla, because Claudius had commanded all the Jews to depart from Rome. He came to them, ³ and because he practiced the same trade, he lived with them and worked,

for by trade they were tent makers. ⁴He reasoned in the synagogue every Sabbath and persuaded Jews and Greeks.

⁵When Silas and Timothy came down from Macedonia, Paul was compelled by the Spirit, testifying to the Jews that Jesus was the Christ. ⁶When they opposed him and blasphemed, he shook out his clothing and said to them, "Your blood be on your own heads! I am clean. From now on, I will go to the Gentiles!"

⁷He departed there and went into the house of a certain man named Justus, one who worshiped God, whose house was next door to the synagogue. ⁸Crispus, the ruler of the synagogue, believed in the Lord with all his house. Many of the Corinthians, when they heard, believed and were baptized.

Responsorial Psalm: Psalms 98: 1-4

¹Sing to Yahweh a new song,
for he has done marvelous things!
His right hand and his holy arm have worked salvation for him.
²Yahweh has made known his salvation.
He has openly shown his righteousness in the sight of the nations.
³He has remembered his loving kindness and his faithfulness toward the house of Israel.
All the ends of the earth have seen the salvation of our God.
⁴Make a joyful noise to Yahweh, all the earth!
Burst out and sing for joy, yes, sing praises!

Gospel: John 16: 16-20

¹⁶ "A little while, and you will not see me. Again a little while, and you will see me."

¹⁷Some of his disciples therefore said to one another, "What is this that he says to us, 'A little while, and you won't see me, and again a little while, and you will see me;' and, 'Because I go to the Father'?" ¹⁸They said therefore, "What is this that he says, 'A little while'? We don't know what he is saying."

¹⁹Therefore Jesus perceived that they wanted to ask him, and he said to them, "Do you inquire among yourselves concerning this, that I said, 'A little while, and you won't see me, and again a little while, and you will see me'? ²⁰ Most certainly I tell you that you will weep and lament, but the world will rejoice. You will be sorrowful, but your sorrow will be turned into joy.

1. Invite the Holy Spirit into this reading, asking the Author of Scripture to speak to you through His Word
2. Read today's passage as many times as you need, take your time
3. Write down (below) what the Lord is saying to you today

_____

_____

Sunday, June 1, 2025
Ascension of the Lord Solemnity (Seventh Sunday of Easter)

First Reading: Acts 1: 1-11

¹ The first book I wrote, Theophilus, concerned all that Jesus began both to do and to teach, ² until the day in which he was received up, after he had given commandment through the Holy Spirit to the apostles whom he had chosen. ³ To these he also showed himself alive after he suffered, by many proofs, appearing to them over a period of forty days and speaking about God's Kingdom. ⁴ Being assembled together with them, he commanded them, "Don't depart from Jerusalem, but wait for the promise of the Father, which you heard from me. ⁵ For John indeed baptized in water, but you will be baptized in the Holy Spirit not many days from now."
⁶ Therefore, when they had come together, they asked him, "Lord, are you now restoring the kingdom to Israel?"
⁷ He said to them, "It isn't for you to know times or seasons which the Father has set within his own authority. ⁸ But you will receive power when the Holy Spirit has come upon you. You will be witnesses to me in Jerusalem, in all Judea and Samaria, and to the uttermost parts of the earth."
⁹ When he had said these things, as they were looking, he was taken up, and a cloud received him out of their sight. ¹⁰ While they were looking steadfastly into the sky as he went, behold,‡ two men stood by them in white clothing, ¹¹ who also said, "You men of Galilee, why do you stand looking into the sky? This Jesus, who was received up from you into the sky, will come back in the same way as you saw him going into the sky."

Responsorial Psalm: Psalms 47: 2-3, 6-7, 8-9

² For Yahweh Most High is awesome.
He is a great King over all the earth.
³ He subdues nations under us,
and peoples under our feet.
⁶ Sing praises to God! Sing praises!
Sing praises to our King! Sing praises!

7 For God is the King of all the earth.
Sing praises with understanding.
8 God reigns over the nations.
God sits on his holy throne.
9 The princes of the peoples are gathered together,
the people of the God of Abraham.
For the shields of the earth belong to God.
He is greatly exalted!

Second Reading: Ephesians 1: 17-23

17 that the God of our Lord Jesus Christ, the Father of glory, may give to you a spirit of wisdom and revelation in the knowledge of him, 18 having the eyes of your hearts‡ enlightened, that you may know what is the hope of his calling, and what are the riches of the glory of his inheritance in the saints, 19 and what is the exceeding greatness of his power toward us who believe, according to that working of the strength of his might 20 which he worked in Christ when he raised him from the dead and made him to sit at his right hand in the heavenly places, 21 far above all rule, authority, power, dominion, and every name that is named, not only in this age, but also in that which is to come. 22 He put all things in subjection under his feet, and gave him to be head over all things for the assembly, 23 which is his body, the fullness of him who fills all in all.

Gospel: Luke 24: 46-53

46 He said to them, "Thus it is written, and thus it was necessary for the Christ to suffer and to rise from the dead the third day, 47 and that repentance and remission of sins should be preached in his name to all the nations, beginning at Jerusalem. 48 You are witnesses of these things. 49 Behold, I send out the promise of my Father on you. But wait in the city of Jerusalem until you are clothed with power from on high."
50 He led them out as far as Bethany, and he lifted up his hands and blessed them. 51 While he blessed them, he withdrew from them and was carried up into heaven. 52 They worshiped him and returned to Jerusalem with great joy, 53 and were continually in the temple, praising and blessing God. Amen.

1. Invite the Holy Spirit into this reading, asking the Author of Scripture to speak to you through His Word
2. Read today's passage as many times as you need, take your time
3. Write down (below) what the Lord is saying to you today
4. Live with this Word in your heart through the day

Sunday, June 8, 2025
PENTECOST SUNDAY

First Reading: Acts 2: 1-11

¹ Now when the day of Pentecost had come, they were all with one accord in one place. ² Suddenly there came from the sky a sound like the rushing of a mighty wind, and it filled all the house where they were sitting. ³ Tongues like fire appeared and were distributed to them, and one sat on each of them. ⁴ They were all filled with the Holy Spirit and began to speak with other languages, as the Spirit gave them the ability to speak.
⁵ Now there were dwelling in Jerusalem Jews, devout men, from every nation under the sky. ⁶ When this sound was heard, the multitude came together and were bewildered, because everyone heard them speaking in his own language. ⁷ They were all amazed and marveled, saying to one another, "Behold, aren't all these who speak Galileans? ⁸ How do we hear, everyone in our own native language? ⁹ Parthians, Medes, Elamites, and people from Mesopotamia, Judea, Cappadocia, Pontus, Asia, ¹⁰ Phrygia, Pamphylia, Egypt, the parts of Libya around Cyrene, visitors from Rome, both Jews and proselytes, ¹¹ Cretans and Arabians—we hear them speaking in our languages the mighty works of God!"

Responsorial Psalm: Psalms 104: 1, 24, 29-30, 31, 34

¹ Bless Yahweh, my soul.
Yahweh, my God, you are very great.
You are clothed with honor and majesty.
²⁴ Yahweh, how many are your works!
In wisdom, you have made them all.
The earth is full of your riches.
²⁹ You hide your face; they are troubled.
You take away their breath; they die and return to the dust.
³⁰ You send out your Spirit and they are created.
You renew the face of the ground.
³¹ Let Yahweh's glory endure forever.
Let Yahweh rejoice in his works.
³⁴ Let my meditation be sweet to him.
I will rejoice in Yahweh.

Second Reading: Romans 8: 8-17

⁸ Those who are in the flesh can't please God.

⁹ But you are not in the flesh but in the Spirit, if it is so that the Spirit of God dwells in you. But if any man doesn't have the Spirit of Christ, he is not his. ¹⁰ If Christ is in you, the body is dead because of sin, but the spirit is alive because of righteousness. ¹¹ But if the Spirit of him who raised up Jesus from the dead dwells in you, he who raised up Christ Jesus from the dead will also give life to your mortal bodies through his Spirit who dwells in you.

¹² So then, brothers, we are debtors, not to the flesh, to live after the flesh. ¹³ For if you live after the flesh, you must die; but if by the Spirit you put to death the deeds of the body, you will live. ¹⁴ For as many as are led by the Spirit of God, these are children of God. ¹⁵ For you didn't receive the spirit of bondage again to fear, but you received the Spirit of adoption, by whom we cry, "Abba!‡ Father!"

¹⁶ The Spirit himself testifies with our spirit that we are children of God; ¹⁷ and if children, then heirs—heirs of God and joint heirs with Christ, if indeed we suffer with him, that we may also be glorified with him.

¹⁸ For I consider that the sufferings of this present time are not worthy to be compared with the glory which will be revealed toward us.

Gospel: John 20: 19-23

¹⁹ When therefore it was evening on that day, the first day of the week, and when the doors were locked where the disciples were assembled, for fear of the Jews, Jesus came and stood in the middle and said to them, "Peace be to you."

²⁰ When he had said this, he showed them his hands and his side. The disciples therefore were glad when they saw the Lord. ²¹ Jesus therefore said to them again, "Peace be to you. As the Father has sent me, even so I send you." ²² When he had said this, he breathed on them, and said to them, "Receive the Holy Spirit! ²³ If you forgive anyone's sins, they have been forgiven them. If you retain anyone's sins, they have been retained."

1. Invite the Holy Spirit into this reading, asking the Author of Scripture to speak to you through His Word
2. Read today's passage as many times as you need, take your time
3. Write down (below) what the Lord is saying to you today
4. Live with this Word in your heart through the day

First Reading: Proverbs 8: 22-31

22 "Yahweh possessed me in the beginning of his work,
before his deeds of old.
23 I was set up from everlasting, from the beginning,
before the earth existed.
24 When there were no depths, I was born,
when there were no springs abounding with water.
25 Before the mountains were settled in place,
before the hills, I was born;
26 while as yet he had not made the earth, nor the fields,
nor the beginning of the dust of the world.
27 When he established the heavens, I was there.
When he set a circle on the surface of the deep,
28 when he established the clouds above,
when the springs of the deep became strong,
29 when he gave to the sea its boundary,
that the waters should not violate his commandment,
when he marked out the foundations of the earth,
30 then I was the craftsman by his side.
I was a delight day by day,
always rejoicing before him,
31 rejoicing in his whole world.
My delight was with the sons of men.

Responsorial Psalm: Psalms 8: 4-9

4 what is man, that you think of him?
What is the son of man, that you care for him?
5 For you have made him a little lower than the angels,‡
and crowned him with glory and honor.
6 You make him ruler over the works of your hands.
You have put all things under his feet:
7 All sheep and cattle,
yes, and the animals of the field,
8 the birds of the sky, the fish of the sea,
and whatever passes through the paths of the seas.
9 Yahweh, our Lord,

how majestic is your name in all the earth!

Second Reading: Romans 5: 1-5

[1] Being therefore justified by faith, we have peace with God through our Lord Jesus Christ; [2] through whom we also have our access by faith into this grace in which we stand. We rejoice in hope of the glory of God. [3] Not only this, but we also rejoice in our sufferings, knowing that suffering produces perseverance; [4] and perseverance, proven character; and proven character, hope; [5] and hope doesn't disappoint us, because God's love has been poured into our hearts through the Holy Spirit who was given to us.

Gospel: John 16: 12-15

[12] "I still have many things to tell you, but you can't bear them now. [13] However, when he, the Spirit of truth, has come, he will guide you into all truth, for he will not speak from himself; but whatever he hears, he will speak. He will declare to you things that are coming. [14] He will glorify me, for he will take from what is mine and will declare it to you. [15] All things that the Father has are mine; therefore I said that he takes‡ of mine and will declare it to you.

1. Invite the Holy Spirit into this reading, asking the Author of Scripture to speak to you through His Word
2. Read today's passage as many times as you need, take your time
3. Write down (below) what the Lord is saying to you today
4. Live with this Word in your heart through the day

Sunday, June 22, 2025
THE MOST HOLY BODY AND BLOOD OF CHRIST
Corpus Christi

First Reading: Genesis 14: 18-20

[18] Melchizedek king of Salem brought out bread and wine. He was priest of God Most High. [19] He blessed him, and said, "Blessed be Abram of God Most High, possessor of

heaven and earth. 20 Blessed be God Most High, who has delivered your enemies into your hand."

Abram gave him a tenth of all.

Responsorial Psalm: Psalms 110: 1, 2, 3, 4

1 Yahweh says to my Lord, "Sit at my right hand,
until I make your enemies your footstool for your feet."
2 Yahweh will send out the rod of your strength out of Zion.
Rule among your enemies.
3 Your people offer themselves willingly in the day of your power, in holy array.
Out of the womb of the morning, you have the dew of your youth.
4 Yahweh has sworn, and will not change his mind:
"You are a priest forever in the order of Melchizedek."

Second Reading: First Corinthians 11: 23-26

23 For I received from the Lord that which also I delivered to you, that the Lord Jesus on the night in which he was betrayed took bread. 24 When he had given thanks, he broke it and said, "Take, eat. This is my body, which is broken for you. Do this in memory of me." 25 In the same way he also took the cup after supper, saying, "This cup is the new covenant in my blood. Do this, as often as you drink, in memory of me." 26 For as often as you eat this bread and drink this cup, you proclaim the Lord's death until he comes.

Gospel: Luke 9: 11b-17

11b He welcomed them, spoke to them of God's Kingdom, and he cured those who needed healing. 12 The day began to wear away; and the twelve came and said to him, "Send the multitude away, that they may go into the surrounding villages and farms and lodge and get food, for we are here in a deserted place."
13 But he said to them, "You give them something to eat."
They said, "We have no more than five loaves and two fish, unless we should go and buy food for all these people." 14 For they were about five thousand men.
He said to his disciples, "Make them sit down in groups of about fifty each." 15 They did so, and made them all sit down. 16 He took the five loaves and the two fish, and looking up to the sky, he blessed them, broke them, and gave them to the disciples to set before the multitude. 17 They ate and were all filled. They gathered up twelve baskets of broken pieces that were left over.

1. Invite the Holy Spirit into this reading, asking the Author of Scripture to speak to you through His Word
2. Read today's passage as many times as you need, take your time
3. Write down (below) what the Lord is saying to you today
4. Live with this Word in your heart through the day

Sunday, June 29, 2025
SAINTS PETER AND PAUL, APOSTLES

First Reading: Acts 12: 1-11

¹ Now about that time, King Herod stretched out his hands to oppress some of the assembly. ² He killed James, the brother of John, with the sword. ³ When he saw that it pleased the Jews, he proceeded to seize Peter also. This was during the days of unleavened bread. ⁴ When he had arrested him, he put him in prison and delivered him to four squads of four soldiers each to guard him, intending to bring him out to the people after the Passover. ⁵ Peter therefore was kept in the prison, but constant prayer was made by the assembly to God for him. ⁶ The same night when Herod was about to bring him out, Peter was sleeping between two soldiers, bound with two chains. Guards in front of the door kept the prison.

⁷ And behold, an angel of the Lord stood by him, and a light shone in the cell. He struck Peter on the side and woke him up, saying, "Stand up quickly!" His chains fell off his hands. ⁸ The angel said to him, "Get dressed and put on your sandals." He did so. He said to him, "Put on your cloak and follow me." ⁹ And he went out and followed him. He didn't know that what was being done by the angel was real, but thought he saw a vision. ¹⁰ When they were past the first and the second guard, they came to the iron gate that leads into the city, which opened to them by itself. They went out and went down one street, and immediately the angel departed from him.

¹¹ When Peter had come to himself, he said, "Now I truly know that the Lord has sent out his angel and delivered me out of the hand of Herod, and from everything the Jewish people were expecting."

Responsorial Psalm: Psalms 34: 2-9

² My soul shall boast in Yahweh.

The humble shall hear of it and be glad.

3 Oh magnify Yahweh with me.

Let's exalt his name together.

4 I sought Yahweh, and he answered me,

and delivered me from all my fears.

5 They looked to him, and were radiant.

Their faces shall never be covered with shame.

6 This poor man cried, and Yahweh heard him,

and saved him out of all his troubles.

7 Yahweh's angel encamps around those who fear him,

and delivers them.

8 Oh taste and see that Yahweh is good.

Blessed is the man who takes refuge in him.

9 Oh fear Yahweh, you his saints,

for there is no lack with those who fear him.

Second Reading: Second Timothy 4: 6-8, 17-18

6 For I am already being offered, and the time of my departure has come. 7 I have fought the good fight. I have finished the course. I have kept the faith. 8 From now on, the crown of righteousness is stored up for me, which the Lord, the righteous judge, will give to me on that day; and not to me only, but also to all those who have loved his appearing.

17 But the Lord stood by me and strengthened me, that through me the message might be fully proclaimed, and that all the Gentiles might hear. So I was delivered out of the mouth of the lion. 18 And the Lord will deliver me from every evil work and will preserve me for his heavenly Kingdom. To him be the glory forever and ever. Amen.

Gospel: Matthew 16: 13-19

13 Now when Jesus came into the parts of Caesarea Philippi, he asked his disciples, saying, "Who do men say that I, the Son of Man, am?"

14 They said, "Some say John the Baptizer, some, Elijah, and others, Jeremiah or one of the prophets."

15 He said to them, "But who do you say that I am?"

16 Simon Peter answered, "You are the Christ, the Son of the living God."

17 Jesus answered him, "Blessed are you, Simon Bar Jonah, for flesh and blood has not revealed this to you, but my Father who is in heaven. 18 I also tell you that you are Peter,‡ and on this rock ‡ I will build my assembly, and the gates of Hades§ will not prevail against it. 19 I will give to you the keys of the Kingdom of Heaven, and whatever you bind

on earth will have been bound in heaven; and whatever you release on earth will have been released in heaven."

1. Invite the Holy Spirit into this reading, asking the Author of Scripture to speak to you through His Word
2. Read today's passage as many times as you need, take your time
3. Write down (below) what the Lord is saying to you today
4. Live with this Word in your heart through the day

Sunday, July 6, 2025
FOURTEENTH SUNDAY IN ORDINARY TIME

First Reading: Isaiah 66: 10-14c

[10] "Rejoice with Jerusalem, and be glad for her, all you who love her.
Rejoice for joy with her, all you who mourn over her;
[11] that you may nurse and be satisfied at the comforting breasts;
that you may drink deeply,
and be delighted with the abundance of her glory."
[12] For Yahweh says, "Behold, I will extend peace to her like a river,
and the glory of the nations like an overflowing stream,
and you will nurse.
You will be carried on her side,
and will be dandled on her knees.
[13] As one whom his mother comforts,
so I will comfort you.
You will be comforted in Jerusalem."
[14] You will see it, and your heart shall rejoice,
and your bones will flourish like the tender grass.
Yahweh's hand will be known among his servants;

Responsorial Psalm: Psalms 66: 1-7, 16 and 20

[1] Make a joyful shout to God, all the earth!
[2] Sing to the glory of his name!

Offer glory and praise!

3 Tell God, "How awesome are your deeds!

Through the greatness of your power, your enemies submit themselves to you.

4 All the earth will worship you,

and will sing to you;

they will sing to your name."

5 Come, and see God's deeds—

awesome work on behalf of the children of men.

6 He turned the sea into dry land.

They went through the river on foot.

There, we rejoiced in him.

7 He rules by his might forever.

His eyes watch the nations.

Don't let the rebellious rise up against him.

16 Come and hear, all you who fear God.

I will declare what he has done for my soul.

20 Blessed be God, who has not turned away my prayer,

nor his loving kindness from me.

Second Reading: Galatians 6: 14-18

14 But far be it from me to boast except in the cross of our Lord Jesus Christ, through which the world has been crucified to me, and I to the world. 15 For in Christ Jesus neither is circumcision anything, nor uncircumcision, but a new creation. 16 As many as walk by this rule, peace and mercy be on them, and on God's Israel.

17 From now on, let no one cause me any trouble, for I bear the marks of the Lord Jesus branded on my body.

18 The grace of our Lord Jesus Christ be with your spirit, brothers. Amen.

Gospel: Luke 10: 1-12, 17-20

1 Now after these things, the Lord also appointed seventy others, and sent them two by two ahead of him‡ into every city and place where he was about to come. 2 Then he said to them, "The harvest is indeed plentiful, but the laborers are few. Pray therefore to the Lord of the harvest, that he may send out laborers into his harvest. 3 Go your ways. Behold, I send you out as lambs among wolves. 4 Carry no purse, nor wallet, nor sandals. Greet no one on the way. 5 Into whatever house you enter, first say, 'Peace be to this house.' 6 If a son of peace is there, your peace will rest on him; but if not, it will return to you. 7 Remain in that same house, eating and drinking the things they give, for the laborer is worthy of his wages. Don't go from house to house. 8 Into whatever city you enter and they receive

you, eat the things that are set before you. 9 Heal the sick who are there and tell them, 'God's Kingdom has come near to you.' 10 But into whatever city you enter and they don't receive you, go out into its streets and say, 11 'Even the dust from your city that clings to us, we wipe off against you. Nevertheless know this, that God's Kingdom has come near to you.' 12 I tell you, it will be more tolerable in that day for Sodom than for that city.

17 The seventy returned with joy, saying, "Lord, even the demons are subject to us in your name!"

18 He said to them, "I saw Satan having fallen like lightning from heaven. 19 Behold, I give you authority to tread on serpents and scorpions, and over all the power of the enemy. Nothing will in any way hurt you. 20 Nevertheless, don't rejoice in this, that the spirits are subject to you, but rejoice that your names are written in heaven."

1. Invite the Holy Spirit into this reading, asking the Author of Scripture to speak to you through His Word
2. Read today's passage as many times as you need, take your time
3. Write down (below) what the Lord is saying to you today
4. Live with this Word in your heart through the day

Sunday, July 13, 2025
FIFTEENTH SUNDAY IN ORDINARY TIME

First Reading: Deuteronomy 30: 10-14

10 if you will obey Yahweh your God's voice, to keep his commandments and his statutes which are written in this book of the law, if you turn to Yahweh your God with all your heart and with all your soul.

11 For this commandment which I command you today is not too hard for you or too distant. 12 It is not in heaven, that you should say, "Who will go up for us to heaven, bring it to us, and proclaim it to us, that we may do it?" 13 Neither is it beyond the sea, that you should say, "Who will go over the sea for us, bring it to us, and proclaim it to us, that we may do it?" 14 But the word is very near to you, in your mouth and in your heart, that you may do it.

Responsorial Psalm: Psalms 19: 8, 9, 10, 11

⁸ Yahweh's precepts are right, rejoicing the heart.

Yahweh's commandment is pure, enlightening the eyes.

⁹ The fear of Yahweh is clean, enduring forever.

Yahweh's ordinances are true, and righteous altogether.

¹⁰ They are more to be desired than gold, yes, than much fine gold,

sweeter also than honey and the extract of the honeycomb.

¹¹ Moreover your servant is warned by them.

In keeping them there is great reward.

Second Reading: Colossians 1: 15-20

¹⁵ He is the image of the invisible God, the firstborn of all creation. ¹⁶ For by him all things were created in the heavens and on the earth, visible things and invisible things, whether thrones or dominions or principalities or powers. All things have been created through him and for him. ¹⁷ He is before all things, and in him all things are held together. ¹⁸ He is the head of the body, the assembly, who is the beginning, the firstborn from the dead, that in all things he might have the preeminence. ¹⁹ For all the fullness was pleased to dwell in him, ²⁰ and through him to reconcile all things to himself by him, whether things on the earth or things in the heavens, having made peace through the blood of his cross.

Gospel: Luke 10: 25-37

²⁵ Behold, a certain lawyer stood up and tested him, saying, "Teacher, what shall I do to inherit eternal life?"

²⁶ He said to him, "What is written in the law? How do you read it?"

²⁷ He answered, "You shall love the Lord your God with all your heart, with all your soul, with all your strength, and with all your mind;* and your neighbor as yourself."*

²⁸ He said to him, "You have answered correctly. Do this, and you will live."

²⁹ But he, desiring to justify himself, asked Jesus, "Who is my neighbor?"

³⁰ Jesus answered, "A certain man was going down from Jerusalem to Jericho, and he fell among robbers, who both stripped him and beat him, and departed, leaving him half dead. ³¹ By chance a certain priest was going down that way. When he saw him, he passed by on the other side. ³² In the same way a Levite also, when he came to the place and saw him, passed by on the other side. ³³ But a certain Samaritan, as he traveled, came where he was. When he saw him, he was moved with compassion, ³⁴ came to him, and bound up his wounds, pouring on oil and wine. He set him on his own animal, brought him to an inn, and took care of him. ³⁵ On the next day, when he departed, he took out two denarii, gave them to the host, and said to him, 'Take care of him. Whatever you spend beyond that, I will repay you when I return.' ³⁶ Now which of these three do you think seemed to be a neighbor to him who fell among the robbers?"

37 He said, "He who showed mercy on him."
Then Jesus said to him, "Go and do likewise."

1. Invite the Holy Spirit into this reading, asking the Author of Scripture to speak to you through His Word
2. Read today's passage as many times as you need, take your time
3. Write down (below) what the Lord is saying to you today
4. Live with this Word in your heart through the day

Sunday, July 20, 2025
SIXTEENTH SUNDAY IN ORDINARY TIME

First Reading: Genesis 18: 1-10a

1 Yahweh appeared to him by the oaks of Mamre, as he sat in the tent door in the heat of the day. 2 He lifted up his eyes and looked, and saw that three men stood near him. When he saw them, he ran to meet them from the tent door, and bowed himself to the earth, 3 and said, "My lord, if now I have found favor in your sight, please don't go away from your servant. 4 Now let a little water be fetched, wash your feet, and rest yourselves under the tree. 5 I will get a piece of bread so you can refresh your heart. After that you may go your way, now that you have come to your servant."
They said, "Very well, do as you have said."
6 Abraham hurried into the tent to Sarah, and said, "Quickly prepare three seahs‡ of fine meal, knead it, and make cakes." 7 Abraham ran to the herd, and fetched a tender and good calf, and gave it to the servant. He hurried to dress it. 8 He took butter, milk, and the calf which he had dressed, and set it before them. He stood by them under the tree, and they ate.
9 They asked him, "Where is Sarah, your wife?"
He said, "There, in the tent."
10a He said, "I will certainly return to you at about this time next year; and behold, Sarah your wife will have a son."

Responsorial Psalm: Psalms 15: 2-5

2 He who walks blamelessly and does what is right,

and speaks truth in his heart;
3 he who doesn't slander with his tongue,
nor does evil to his friend,
nor casts slurs against his fellow man;
4 in whose eyes a vile man is despised,
but who honors those who fear Yahweh;
he who keeps an oath even when it hurts, and doesn't change;
5 he who doesn't lend out his money for usury,
nor take a bribe against the innocent.
He who does these things shall never be shaken.

Second Reading: Colossians 1: 24-28

24 Now I rejoice in my sufferings for your sake, and fill up on my part that which is lacking of the afflictions of Christ in my flesh for his body's sake, which is the assembly, 25 of which I was made a servant according to the stewardship of God which was given me toward you to fulfill the word of God, 26 the mystery which has been hidden for ages and generations. But now it has been revealed to his saints, 27 to whom God was pleased to make known what are the riches of the glory of this mystery among the Gentiles, which is Christ in you, the hope of glory. 28 We proclaim him, admonishing every man and teaching every man in all wisdom, that we may present every man perfect in Christ Jesus;

Gospel: Luke 10: 38-42

38 As they went on their way, he entered into a certain village, and a certain woman named Martha received him into her house. 39 She had a sister called Mary, who also sat at Jesus' feet and heard his word. 40 But Martha was distracted with much serving, and she came up to him, and said, "Lord, don't you care that my sister left me to serve alone? Ask her therefore to help me."
41 Jesus answered her, "Martha, Martha, you are anxious and troubled about many things, 42 but one thing is needed. Mary has chosen the good part, which will not be taken away from her."

1. Invite the Holy Spirit into this reading, asking the Author of Scripture to speak to you through His Word
2. Read today's passage as many times as you need, take your time
3. Write down (below) what the Lord is saying to you today
4. Live with this Word in your heart through the day

Sunday, July 27, 2025
SEVENTEENTH SUNDAY IN ORDINARY TIME

First Reading: Genesis 18: 20-32

20 Yahweh said, "Because the cry of Sodom and Gomorrah is great, and because their sin is very grievous, 21 I will go down now, and see whether their deeds are as bad as the reports which have come to me. If not, I will know."

22 The men turned from there, and went toward Sodom, but Abraham stood yet before Yahweh. 23 Abraham came near, and said, "Will you consume the righteous with the wicked? 24 What if there are fifty righteous within the city? Will you consume and not spare the place for the fifty righteous who are in it? 25 May it be far from you to do things like that, to kill the righteous with the wicked, so that the righteous should be like the wicked. May that be far from you. Shouldn't the Judge of all the earth do right?"

26 Yahweh said, "If I find in Sodom fifty righteous within the city, then I will spare the whole place for their sake." 27 Abraham answered, "See now, I have taken it on myself to speak to the Lord, although I am dust and ashes. 28 What if there will lack five of the fifty righteous? Will you destroy all the city for lack of five?"

He said, "I will not destroy it if I find forty-five there."

29 He spoke to him yet again, and said, "What if there are forty found there?"

He said, "I will not do it for the forty's sake."

30 He said, "Oh don't let the Lord be angry, and I will speak. What if there are thirty found there?"

He said, "I will not do it if I find thirty there."

31 He said, "See now, I have taken it on myself to speak to the Lord. What if there are twenty found there?"

He said, "I will not destroy it for the twenty's sake."

32 He said, "Oh don't let the Lord be angry, and I will speak just once more. What if ten are found there?"

He said, "I will not destroy it for the ten's sake."

Responsorial Psalm: Psalms 138: 1-2, 2-3, 6-7, 7-8

1 I will give you thanks with my whole heart.
Before the gods,⸵ I will sing praises to you.

2 I will bow down toward your holy temple,
and give thanks to your Name for your loving kindness and for your truth;
for you have exalted your Name and your Word above all.
3 In the day that I called, you answered me.
You encouraged me with strength in my soul.
6 For though Yahweh is high, yet he looks after the lowly;
but he knows the proud from afar.
7 Though I walk in the middle of trouble, you will revive me.
You will stretch out your hand against the wrath of my enemies.
Your right hand will save me.
8 Yahweh will fulfill that which concerns me.
Your loving kindness, Yahweh, endures forever.
Don't forsake the works of your own hands.

Second Reading: Colossians 2: 12-14

12 having been buried with him in baptism, in which you were also raised with him through faith in the working of God, who raised him from the dead. 13 You were dead through your trespasses and the uncircumcision of your flesh. He made you alive together with him, having forgiven us all our trespasses, 14 wiping out the handwriting in ordinances which was against us. He has taken it out of the way, nailing it to the cross.

Gospel: Luke 11: 1-13

1 When he finished praying in a certain place, one of his disciples said to him, "Lord, teach us to pray, just as John also taught his disciples."
2 He said to them, "When you pray, say,
'Our Father in heaven,
may your name be kept holy.
May your Kingdom come.
May your will be done on earth, as it is in heaven.
3 Give us day by day our daily bread.
4 Forgive us our sins,
for we ourselves also forgive everyone who is indebted to us.
Bring us not into temptation,
but deliver us from the evil one.' "
5 He said to them, "Which of you, if you go to a friend at midnight and tell him, 'Friend, lend me three loaves of bread, 6 for a friend of mine has come to me from a journey, and I have nothing to set before him,' 7 and he from within will answer and say, 'Don't bother me. The door is now shut, and my children are with me in bed. I can't get up and give it to

you'? ⁸ I tell you, although he will not rise and give it to him because he is his friend, yet because of his persistence, he will get up and give him as many as he needs.

⁹ "I tell you, keep asking, and it will be given you. Keep seeking, and you will find. Keep knocking, and it will be opened to you. ¹⁰ For everyone who asks receives. He who seeks finds. To him who knocks it will be opened.

¹¹ "Which of you fathers, if your son asks for bread, will give him a stone? Or if he asks for a fish, he won't give him a snake instead of a fish, will he? ¹² Or if he asks for an egg, he won't give him a scorpion, will he? ¹³ If you then, being evil, know how to give good gifts to your children, how much more will your heavenly Father give the Holy Spirit to those who ask him?"

1. Invite the Holy Spirit into this reading, asking the Author of Scripture to speak to you through His Word
2. Read today's passage as many times as you need, take your time
3. Write down (below) what the Lord is saying to you today
4. Live with this Word in your heart through the day

_____

_____

Sunday, August 3, 2025
EIGHTEENTH SUNDAY IN ORDINARY TIME

First Reading: Ecclesiastes 1: 2; 2: 21-23

² "Vanity of vanities," says the Preacher; "Vanity of vanities, all is vanity."
²¹ For there is a man whose labor is with wisdom, with knowledge, and with skillfulness; yet he shall leave it for his portion to a man who has not labored for it. This also is vanity and a great evil. ²² For what does a man have of all his labor and of the striving of his heart, in which he labors under the sun? ²³ For all his days are sorrows, and his travail is grief; yes, even in the night his heart takes no rest. This also is vanity.

Responsorial Psalm: Psalms 90: 3-6, 12-14 and 17

³ You turn man to destruction, saying,
"Return, you children of men."
⁴ For a thousand years in your sight are just like yesterday when it is past,
like a watch in the night.

⁵ You sweep them away as they sleep.
In the morning they sprout like new grass.
⁶ In the morning it sprouts and springs up.
By evening, it is withered and dry.
¹² So teach us to count our days,
that we may gain a heart of wisdom.
¹³ Relent, Yahweh!§
How long?
Have compassion on your servants!
¹⁴ Satisfy us in the morning with your loving kindness,
that we may rejoice and be glad all our days.
¹⁷ Let the favor of the Lord our God be on us.
Establish the work of our hands for us.
Yes, establish the work of our hands.

Second Reading: Colossians 3: 1-5, 9-11

¹ If then you were raised together with Christ, seek the things that are above, where Christ is, seated on the right hand of God. ² Set your mind on the things that are above, not on the things that are on the earth. ³ For you died, and your life is hidden with Christ in God. ⁴ When Christ, our life, is revealed, then you will also be revealed with him in glory.
⁵ Put to death therefore your members which are on the earth: sexual immorality, uncleanness, depraved passion, evil desire, and covetousness, which is idolatry.
⁹ Don't lie to one another, seeing that you have put off the old man with his doings, ¹⁰ and have put on the new man, who is being renewed in knowledge after the image of his Creator, ¹¹ where there can't be Greek and Jew, circumcision and uncircumcision, barbarian, Scythian, bondservant, or free person; but Christ is all, and in all.

Gospel: Luke 12: 13-21

¹³ One of the multitude said to him, "Teacher, tell my brother to divide the inheritance with me."
¹⁴ But he said to him, "Man, who made me a judge or an arbitrator over you?" ¹⁵ He said to them, "Beware! Keep yourselves from covetousness, for a man's life doesn't consist of the abundance of the things which he possesses."
¹⁶ He spoke a parable to them, saying, "The ground of a certain rich man produced abundantly. ¹⁷ He reasoned within himself, saying, 'What will I do, because I don't have room to store my crops?' ¹⁸ He said, 'This is what I will do. I will pull down my barns, build bigger ones, and there I will store all my grain and my goods. ¹⁹ I will tell my soul, "Soul, you have many goods laid up for many years. Take your ease, eat, drink, and be merry." '

²⁰ "But God said to him, 'You foolish one, tonight your soul is required of you. The things which you have prepared—whose will they be?' ²¹ So is he who lays up treasure for himself, and is not rich toward God."

1. Invite the Holy Spirit into this reading, asking the Author of Scripture to speak to you through His Word
2. Read today's passage as many times as you need, take your time
3. Write down (below) what the Lord is saying to you today
4. Live with this Word in your heart through the day

Sunday, August 10, 2025
NINETEENTH SUNDAY IN ORDINARY TIME

First Reading: Wisdom 18: 6-9

⁶ Our fathers were made aware of that night beforehand,
that, having sure knowledge, they might be cheered by the oaths which they had trusted.
⁷ Salvation of the righteous and destruction of the enemies was expected by your people.
⁸ For as you took vengeance on the adversaries,
by the same means, calling us to yourself, you glorified us.
⁹ For holy children of good men offered sacrifice in secret,
and with one consent they agreed to the covenant of the divine law,
that they would partake alike in the same good things and the same perils,
the fathers already leading the sacred songs of praise.

Responsorial Psalm: Psalms 33: 1, 12, 18-22

¹ Rejoice in Yahweh, you righteous!
Praise is fitting for the upright.
¹² Blessed is the nation whose God is Yahweh,
the people whom he has chosen for his own inheritance.
¹⁸ Behold, Yahweh's eye is on those who fear him,
on those who hope in his loving kindness,
¹⁹ to deliver their soul from death,
to keep them alive in famine.

²⁰ Our soul has waited for Yahweh.

He is our help and our shield.

²¹ For our heart rejoices in him,

because we have trusted in his holy name.

²² Let your loving kindness be on us, Yahweh,

since we have hoped in you.

Second Reading: Hebrews 11: 1-2, 8-12

¹ Now faith is assurance of things hoped for, proof of things not seen. ² For by this, the elders obtained approval.

⁸ By faith Abraham, when he was called, obeyed to go out to the place which he was to receive for an inheritance. He went out, not knowing where he went. ⁹ By faith he lived as an alien in the land of promise, as in a land not his own, dwelling in tents with Isaac and Jacob, the heirs with him of the same promise. ¹⁰ For he was looking for the city which has foundations, whose builder and maker is God.

¹¹ By faith even Sarah herself received power to conceive, and she bore a child when she was past age, since she counted him faithful who had promised. ¹² Therefore as many as the stars of the sky in multitude, and as innumerable as the sand which is by the sea shore, were fathered by one man, and him as good as dead.

Gospel: Luke 12: 32-48

³² "Don't be afraid, little flock, for it is your Father's good pleasure to give you the Kingdom. ³³ Sell what you have and give gifts to the needy. Make for yourselves purses which don't grow old, a treasure in the heavens that doesn't fail, where no thief approaches and no moth destroys. ³⁴ For where your treasure is, there will your heart be also.

³⁵ "Let your waist be dressed and your lamps burning. ³⁶ Be like men watching for their lord when he returns from the wedding feast, that when he comes and knocks, they may immediately open to him. ³⁷ Blessed are those servants whom the lord will find watching when he comes. Most certainly I tell you that he will dress himself, make them recline, and will come and serve them. ³⁸ They will be blessed if he comes in the second or third watch and finds them so. ³⁹ But know this, that if the master of the house had known in what hour the thief was coming, he would have watched and not allowed his house to be broken into. ⁴⁰ Therefore be ready also, for the Son of Man is coming in an hour that you don't expect him."

⁴¹ Peter said to him, "Lord, are you telling this parable to us, or to everybody?"

⁴² The Lord said, "Who then is the faithful and wise steward, whom his lord will set over his household, to give them their portion of food at the right times? ⁴³ Blessed is that servant whom his lord will find doing so when he comes. ⁴⁴ Truly I tell you that he will set

him over all that he has. 45 But if that servant says in his heart, 'My lord delays his coming,' and begins to beat the menservants and the maidservants, and to eat and drink and to be drunken, 46 then the lord of that servant will come in a day when he isn't expecting him and in an hour that he doesn't know, and will cut him in two, and place his portion with the unfaithful. 47 That servant who knew his lord's will, and didn't prepare nor do what he wanted, will be beaten with many stripes, 48 but he who didn't know, and did things worthy of stripes, will be beaten with few stripes. To whomever much is given, of him will much be required; and to whom much was entrusted, of him more will be asked.

1. Invite the Holy Spirit into this reading, asking the Author of Scripture to speak to you through His Word
2. Read today's passage as many times as you need, take your time
3. Write down (below) what the Lord is saying to you today
4. Live with this Word in your heart through the day

Sunday, August 17, 2025
TWENTIETH SUNDAY IN ORDINARY TIME

First Reading: Jeremiah 38: 4-6, 8-10

4 Then the princes said to the king, "Please let this man be put to death, because he weakens the hands of the men of war who remain in this city, and the hands of all the people, in speaking such words to them; for this man doesn't seek the welfare of this people, but harm."

5 Zedekiah the king said, "Behold, he is in your hand; for the king can't do anything to oppose you."

6 Then they took Jeremiah and threw him into the dungeon of Malchijah the king's son, that was in the court of the guard. They let down Jeremiah with cords. In the dungeon there was no water, but mire; and Jeremiah sank in the mire.

8 Ebedmelech went out of the king's house, and spoke to the king, saying, 9 "My lord the king, these men have done evil in all that they have done to Jeremiah the prophet, whom they have cast into the dungeon. He is likely to die in the place where he is, because of the famine; for there is no more bread in the city."

10 Then the king commanded Ebedmelech the Ethiopian, saying, "Take from here thirty men with you, and take up Jeremiah the prophet out of the dungeon, before he dies."

Responsorial Psalm: Psalms 40: 2, 3, 4

2 He brought me up also out of a horrible pit,
out of the miry clay.
He set my feet on a rock,
and gave me a firm place to stand.
3 He has put a new song in my mouth, even praise to our God.
Many shall see it, and fear, and shall trust in Yahweh.
4 Blessed is the man who makes Yahweh his trust,
and doesn't respect the proud, nor such as turn away to lies.

Second Reading: Hebrews 12: 1-4

1 Therefore let's also, seeing we are surrounded by so great a cloud of witnesses, lay aside every weight and the sin which so easily entangles us, and let's run with perseverance the race that is set before us, 2 looking to Jesus, the author and perfecter of faith, who for the joy that was set before him endured the cross, despising its shame, and has sat down at the right hand of the throne of God.
3 For consider him who has endured such contradiction of sinners against himself, that you don't grow weary, fainting in your souls. 4 You have not yet resisted to blood, striving against sin.

Gospel: Luke 12: 49-53

49 "I came to throw fire on the earth. I wish it were already kindled. 50 But I have a baptism to be baptized with, and how distressed I am until it is accomplished! 51 Do you think that I have come to give peace in the earth? I tell you, no, but rather division. 52 For from now on, there will be five in one house divided, three against two, and two against three. 53 They will be divided, father against son, and son against father; mother against daughter, and daughter against her mother; mother-in-law against her daughter-in-law, and daughter-in-law against her mother-in-law."

1. Invite the Holy Spirit into this reading, asking the Author of Scripture to speak to you through His Word
2. Read today's passage as many times as you need, take your time
3. Write down (below) what the Lord is saying to you today
4. Live with this Word in your heart through the day

Sunday, August 24, 2025
TWENTY-FIRST SUNDAY IN ORDINARY TIME

First Reading: Isaiah 66: 18-21

[18] "For I know their works and their thoughts. The time comes that I will gather all nations and languages, and they will come, and will see my glory.
[19] "I will set a sign among them, and I will send those who escape of them to the nations, to Tarshish, Pul, and Lud, who draw the bow, to Tubal and Javan, to far-away islands, who have not heard my fame, nor have seen my glory; and they shall declare my glory among the nations. [20] They shall bring all your brothers out of all the nations for an offering to Yahweh, on horses, in chariots, in litters, on mules, and on camels, to my holy mountain Jerusalem, says Yahweh, as the children of Israel bring their offering in a clean vessel into Yahweh's house. [21] Of them I will also select priests and Levites," says Yahweh.

Responsorial Psalm: Psalms 117: 1, 2

[1] Praise Yahweh, all you nations!
Extol him, all you peoples!
[2] For his loving kindness is great toward us.
Yahweh's faithfulness endures forever.
Praise Yah!

Second Reading: Hebrews 12: 5-7, 11-13

[5] You have forgotten the exhortation which reasons with you as with children,
"My son, don't take lightly the chastening of the Lord,
nor faint when you are reproved by him;
[6] for whom the Lord loves, he disciplines,
and chastises every son whom he receives."[*]
[7] It is for discipline that you endure. God deals with you as with children, for what son is there whom his father doesn't discipline?
[11] All chastening seems for the present to be not joyous but grievous; yet afterward it yields the peaceful fruit of righteousness to those who have been trained by it. [12] Therefore lift up

the hands that hang down and the feeble knees, * 13 and make straight paths for your feet,* so what is lame may not be dislocated, but rather be healed.

Gospel: Luke 13: 22-30

22 He went on his way through cities and villages, teaching, and traveling on to Jerusalem. 23 One said to him, "Lord, are they few who are saved?"
He said to them, 24 "Strive to enter in by the narrow door, for many, I tell you, will seek to enter in and will not be able. 25 When once the master of the house has risen up and has shut the door, and you begin to stand outside and to knock at the door, saying, 'Lord, Lord, open to us!' then he will answer and tell you, 'I don't know you or where you come from.' 26 Then you will begin to say, 'We ate and drank in your presence, and you taught in our streets.' 27 He will say, 'I tell you, I don't know where you come from. Depart from me, all you workers of iniquity.' 28 There will be weeping and gnashing of teeth when you see Abraham, Isaac, Jacob, and all the prophets in God's Kingdom, and yourselves being thrown outside. 29 They will come from the east, west, north, and south, and will sit down in God's Kingdom. 30 Behold, there are some who are last who will be first, and there are some who are first who will be last."

1. Invite the Holy Spirit into this reading, asking the Author of Scripture to speak to you through His Word
2. Read today's passage as many times as you need, take your time
3. Write down (below) what the Lord is saying to you today
4. Live with this Word in your heart through the day

_____

_____

Sunday, August 31, 2025
TWENTY-SECOND SUNDAY IN ORDINARY TIME

First Reading: Sirach 3: 17-18, 20, 28-29

17 My son, go on with your business in humility;
so you will be loved by an acceptable man.
18 The greater you are, humble yourself the more,
and you will find favor before the Lord.
20 For the power of the Lord is great,

and he is glorified by those who are lowly.
28 The calamity of the proud has no healing,
for a weed of wickedness has taken root in him.
29 The heart of the prudent will understand a proverb.
A wise man desires the ear of a listener.

Responsorial Psalm: Psalms 68: 4-7, 10-11

4 Sing to God! Sing praises to his name!
Extol him who rides on the clouds:
to Yah, his name!
Rejoice before him!
5 A father of the fatherless, and a defender of the widows,
is God in his holy habitation.
6 God sets the lonely in families.
He brings out the prisoners with singing,
but the rebellious dwell in a sun-scorched land.
7 God, when you went out before your people,
when you marched through the wilderness...
Selah.
10 Your congregation lived therein.
You, God, prepared your goodness for the poor.
11 The Lord announced the word.
The ones who proclaim it are a great company.

Second Reading: Hebrews 12: 18-19, 22-24

18 For you have not come to a mountain that might be touched and that burned with fire, and to blackness, darkness, storm, 19 the sound of a trumpet, and the voice of words; which those who heard it begged that not one more word should be spoken to them,
22 But you have come to Mount Zion and to the city of the living God, the heavenly Jerusalem, and to innumerable multitudes of angels, 23 to the festal gathering and assembly of the firstborn who are enrolled in heaven, to God the Judge of all, to the spirits of just men made perfect, 24 to Jesus, the mediator of a new covenant,* and to the blood of sprinkling that speaks better than that of Abel.

Gospel: Luke 14: 1, 7-14

1 When he went into the house of one of the rulers of the Pharisees on a Sabbath to eat bread, they were watching him.

7 He spoke a parable to those who were invited, when he noticed how they chose the best seats, and said to them, 8 "When you are invited by anyone to a wedding feast, don't sit in the best seat, since perhaps someone more honorable than you might be invited by him, 9 and he who invited both of you would come and tell you, 'Make room for this person.' Then you would begin, with shame, to take the lowest place. 10 But when you are invited, go and sit in the lowest place, so that when he who invited you comes, he may tell you, 'Friend, move up higher.' Then you will be honored in the presence of all who sit at the table with you. 11 For everyone who exalts himself will be humbled, and whoever humbles himself will be exalted."

12 He also said to the one who had invited him, "When you make a dinner or a supper, don't call your friends, nor your brothers, nor your kinsmen, nor rich neighbors, or perhaps they might also return the favor, and pay you back. 13 But when you make a feast, ask the poor, the maimed, the lame, or the blind; 14 and you will be blessed, because they don't have the resources to repay you. For you will be repaid in the resurrection of the righteous."

1. Invite the Holy Spirit into this reading, asking the Author of Scripture to speak to you through His Word
2. Read today's passage as many times as you need, take your time
3. Write down (below) what the Lord is saying to you today
4. Live with this Word in your heart through the day

_____

_____

Sunday, September 7, 2025
TWENTY-THIRD SUNDAY IN ORDINARY TIME

First Reading: Wisdom 9: 13-18b

13 For what man will know the counsel of God?
Or who will conceive what the Lord wills?
14 For the thoughts of mortals are unstable,
and our plans are prone to fail.
15 For a corruptible body weighs down the soul.
The earthy tent burdens a mind that is full of cares.
16 We can hardly guess the things that are on earth,
and we find the things that are close at hand with labor;
but who has traced out the things that are in the heavens?

17 Who gained knowledge of your counsel, unless you gave wisdom,
and sent your holy spirit from on high?
18 It was thus that the ways of those who are on earth were corrected,
and men were taught the things that are pleasing to you.

Responsorial Psalm: Psalms 90: 3-6, 12-14 and 17

3 You turn man to destruction, saying,
"Return, you children of men."
4 For a thousand years in your sight are just like yesterday when it is past,
like a watch in the night.
5 You sweep them away as they sleep.
In the morning they sprout like new grass.
6 In the morning it sprouts and springs up.
By evening, it is withered and dry.
12 So teach us to count our days,
that we may gain a heart of wisdom.
13 Relent, Yahweh!§
How long?
Have compassion on your servants!
14 Satisfy us in the morning with your loving kindness,
that we may rejoice and be glad all our days.
17 Let the favor of the Lord our God be on us.
Establish the work of our hands for us.
Yes, establish the work of our hands.

Second Reading: Philemon 1: 9-10, 12-17

9 yet for love's sake I rather appeal to you, being such a one as Paul, the aged, but also a prisoner of Jesus Christ. 10 I appeal to you for my child Onesimus, whom I have become the father of in my chains,‡
12 I am sending him back. Therefore receive him, that is, my own heart, 13 whom I desired to keep with me, that on your behalf he might serve me in my chains for the Good News. 14 But I was willing to do nothing without your consent, that your goodness would not be as of necessity, but of free will. 15 For perhaps he was therefore separated from you for a while that you would have him forever, 16 no longer as a slave, but more than a slave, a beloved brother—especially to me, but how much rather to you, both in the flesh and in the Lord.
17 If then you count me a partner, receive him as you would receive me.

Gospel: Luke 14: 25-33

25 Now great multitudes were going with him. He turned and said to them, 26 "If anyone comes to me, and doesn't disregard§ his own father, mother, wife, children, brothers, and sisters, yes, and his own life also, he can't be my disciple. 27 Whoever doesn't bear his own cross and come after me, can't be my disciple. 28 For which of you, desiring to build a tower, doesn't first sit down and count the cost, to see if he has enough to complete it? 29 Or perhaps, when he has laid a foundation and isn't able to finish, everyone who sees begins to mock him, 30 saying, 'This man began to build and wasn't able to finish.' 31 Or what king, as he goes to encounter another king in war, will not sit down first and consider whether he is able with ten thousand to meet him who comes against him with twenty thousand? 32 Or else, while the other is yet a great way off, he sends an envoy and asks for conditions of peace. 33 So therefore, whoever of you who doesn't renounce all that he has, he can't be my disciple.

1. Invite the Holy Spirit into this reading, asking the Author of Scripture to speak to you through His Word
2. Read today's passage as many times as you need, take your time
3. Write down (below) what the Lord is saying to you today
4. Live with this Word in your heart through the day

_____

_____

Sunday, September 14, 2025
THE EXALTATION OF THE HOLY CROSS

First Reading: Numbers 21: 4b-9

4b The soul of the people was very discouraged because of the journey. 5 The people spoke against God and against Moses: "Why have you brought us up out of Egypt to die in the wilderness? For there is no bread, there is no water, and our soul loathes this disgusting food!"
6 Yahweh sent venomous snakes among the people, and they bit the people. Many people of Israel died. 7 The people came to Moses, and said, "We have sinned, because we have spoken against Yahweh and against you. Pray to Yahweh, that he take away the serpents from us." Moses prayed for the people.

⁸ Yahweh said to Moses, "Make a venomous snake, and set it on a pole. It shall happen that everyone who is bitten, when he sees it, shall live." ⁹ Moses made a serpent of bronze, and set it on the pole. If a serpent had bitten any man, when he looked at the serpent of bronze, he lived.

Responsorial Psalm: Psalms 78: 1bc-2, 34-38

¹ Hear my teaching, my people.
Turn your ears to the words of my mouth.
² I will open my mouth in a parable.
I will utter dark sayings of old,
³⁴ When he killed them, then they inquired after him.
They returned and sought God earnestly.
³⁵ They remembered that God was their rock,
the Most High God, their redeemer.
³⁶ But they flattered him with their mouth,
and lied to him with their tongue.
³⁷ For their heart was not right with him,
neither were they faithful in his covenant.
³⁸ But he, being merciful, forgave iniquity, and didn't destroy them.
Yes, many times he turned his anger away,
and didn't stir up all his wrath.

Second Reading: Philippians 2: 6-11

⁶ who, existing in the form of God, didn't consider equality with God a thing to be grasped, ⁷ but emptied himself, taking the form of a servant, being made in the likeness of men. ⁸ And being found in human form, he humbled himself, becoming obedient to the point of death, yes, the death of the cross. ⁹ Therefore God also highly exalted him, and gave to him the name which is above every name, ¹⁰ that at the name of Jesus every knee should bow, of those in heaven, those on earth, and those under the earth, ¹¹ and that every tongue should confess that Jesus Christ is Lord, to the glory of God the Father.

Gospel: John 3: 13-17

¹³ No one has ascended into heaven but he who descended out of heaven, the Son of Man, who is in heaven. ¹⁴ As Moses lifted up the serpent in the wilderness, even so must the Son of Man be lifted up, ¹⁵ that whoever believes in him should not perish, but have eternal life. ¹⁶ For God so loved the world, that he gave his only born§ Son, that whoever believes

in him should not perish, but have eternal life. ¹⁷ For God didn't send his Son into the world to judge the world, but that the world should be saved through him.

1. Invite the Holy Spirit into this reading, asking the Author of Scripture to speak to you through His Word
2. Read today's passage as many times as you need, take your time
3. Write down (below) what the Lord is saying to you today
4. Live with this Word in your heart through the day

Sunday, September 21, 2025
TWENTY-FIFTH SUNDAY IN OPRDINARY TIME

First Reading: Amos 8: 4-7

⁴ Hear this, you who desire to swallow up the needy,
and cause the poor of the land to fail,
⁵ saying, 'When will the new moon be gone, that we may sell grain?
And the Sabbath, that we may market wheat,
making the ephah⁺ small, and the shekel⁺ large,
and dealing falsely with balances of deceit;
⁶ that we may buy the poor for silver,
and the needy for a pair of sandals,
and sell the sweepings with the wheat?' "
⁷ Yahweh has sworn by the pride of Jacob,
"Surely I will never forget any of their works.

Responsorial Psalm: Psalms 113: 1-2, 4-6, 7-8

¹ Praise Yah!
Praise, you servants of Yahweh,
praise Yahweh's name.
² Blessed be Yahweh's name,
from this time forward and forever more.
⁴ Yahweh is high above all nations,
his glory above the heavens.

5 Who is like Yahweh, our God,
who has his seat on high,
6 who stoops down to see in heaven and in the earth?
7 He raises up the poor out of the dust,
and lifts up the needy from the ash heap,
8 that he may set him with princes,
even with the princes of his people.

Second Reading: First Timothy 2: 1-8

1 I exhort therefore, first of all, that petitions, prayers, intercessions, and givings of thanks be made for all men, 2 for kings and all who are in high places, that we may lead a tranquil and quiet life in all godliness and reverence. 3 For this is good and acceptable in the sight of God our Savior, 4 who desires all people to be saved and come to full knowledge of the truth. 5 For there is one God and one mediator between God and men, the man Christ Jesus, 6 who gave himself as a ransom for all, the testimony at the proper time, 7 to which I was appointed a preacher and an apostle—I am telling the truth in Christ, not lying—a teacher of the Gentiles in faith and truth.
8 I desire therefore that the men in every place pray, lifting up holy hands without anger and doubting.

Gospel: Luke 16: 1-13

1 He also said to his disciples, "There was a certain rich man who had a manager. An accusation was made to him that this man was wasting his possessions. 2 He called him, and said to him, 'What is this that I hear about you? Give an accounting of your management, for you can no longer be manager.'
3 "The manager said within himself, 'What will I do, seeing that my lord is taking away the management position from me? I don't have strength to dig. I am ashamed to beg. 4 I know what I will do, so that when I am removed from management, they may receive me into their houses.' 5 Calling each one of his lord's debtors to him, he said to the first, 'How much do you owe to my lord?' 6 He said, 'A hundred batos‡ of oil.' He said to him, 'Take your bill, and sit down quickly and write fifty.' 7 Then he said to another, 'How much do you owe?' He said, 'A hundred cors‡ of wheat.' He said to him, 'Take your bill, and write eighty.'
8 "His lord commended the dishonest manager because he had done wisely, for the children of this world are, in their own generation, wiser than the children of the light. 9 I tell you, make for yourselves friends by means of unrighteous mammon, so that when you fail, they may receive you into the eternal tents. 10 He who is faithful in a very little is faithful also in much. He who is dishonest in a very little is also dishonest in much. 11 If therefore you have not been faithful in the unrighteous mammon, who will commit to your

trust the true riches? ¹² If you have not been faithful in that which is another's, who will give you that which is your own? ¹³ No servant can serve two masters, for either he will hate the one and love the other; or else he will hold to one and despise the other. You aren't able to serve God and Mammon."

1. Invite the Holy Spirit into this reading, asking the Author of Scripture to speak to you through His Word
2. Read today's passage as many times as you need, take your time
3. Write down (below) what the Lord is saying to you today
4. Live with this Word in your heart through the day

Sunday, September 28, 2025
TWENTY-SIXTH SUNDAY IN ORDINARY TIME

First Reading: Amos 6: 1a, 4-7

¹ᵃ Woe to those who are at ease in Zion,
⁴ who lie on beds of ivory,
and stretch themselves on their couches,
and eat the lambs out of the flock,
and the calves out of the middle of the stall,
⁵ who strum on the strings of a harp,
who invent for themselves instruments of music, like David;
⁶ who drink wine in bowls,
and anoint themselves with the best oils,
but they are not grieved for the affliction of Joseph.
⁷ Therefore they will now go captive with the first who go captive.
The feasting and lounging will end.

Responsorial Psalm: Psalms 146: 7, 8-9, 9-10

⁷ who executes justice for the oppressed;
who gives food to the hungry.
Yahweh frees the prisoners.
⁸ Yahweh opens the eyes of the blind.

Yahweh raises up those who are bowed down.
Yahweh loves the righteous.
9 Yahweh preserves the foreigners.
He upholds the fatherless and widow,
but he turns the way of the wicked upside down.
10 Yahweh will reign forever;
your God, O Zion, to all generations.
Praise Yah!

Second Reading: First Timothy 6: 11-16

11 But you, man of God, flee these things, and follow after righteousness, godliness, faith, love, perseverance, and gentleness. 12 Fight the good fight of faith. Take hold of the eternal life to which you were called, and you confessed the good confession in the sight of many witnesses. 13 I command you before God who gives life to all things, and before Christ Jesus who before Pontius Pilate testified the good confession, 14 that you keep the commandment without spot, blameless until the appearing of our Lord Jesus Christ, 15 which at the right time he will show, who is the blessed and only Ruler, the King of kings and Lord of lords. 16 He alone has immortality, dwelling in unapproachable light, whom no man has seen nor can see, to whom be honor and eternal power. Amen.

Gospel: Luke 16: 19-31

19 "Now there was a certain rich man, and he was clothed in purple and fine linen, living in luxury every day. 20 A certain beggar, named Lazarus, was taken to his gate, full of sores, 21 and desiring to be fed with the crumbs that fell from the rich man's table. Yes, even the dogs came and licked his sores. 22 The beggar died, and he was carried away by the angels to Abraham's bosom. The rich man also died and was buried. 23 In Hades,‡ he lifted up his eyes, being in torment, and saw Abraham far off, and Lazarus at his bosom. 24 He cried and said, 'Father Abraham, have mercy on me, and send Lazarus, that he may dip the tip of his finger in water and cool my tongue! For I am in anguish in this flame.'
25 "But Abraham said, 'Son, remember that you, in your lifetime, received your good things, and Lazarus, in the same way, bad things. But here he is now comforted and you are in anguish. 26 Besides all this, between us and you there is a great gulf fixed, that those who want to pass from here to you are not able, and that no one may cross over from there to us.'
27 "He said, 'I ask you therefore, father, that you would send him to my father's house— 28 for I have five brothers—that he may testify to them, so they won't also come into this place of torment.'

²⁹ "But Abraham said to him, 'They have Moses and the prophets. Let them listen to them.'
³⁰ "He said, 'No, father Abraham, but if one goes to them from the dead, they will repent.'
³¹ "He said to him, 'If they don't listen to Moses and the prophets, neither will they be persuaded if one rises from the dead.' "

1. Invite the Holy Spirit into this reading, asking the Author of Scripture to speak to you through His Word
2. Read today's passage as many times as you need, take your time
3. Write down (below) what the Lord is saying to you today
4. Live with this Word in your heart through the day

Sunday, October 5, 2025
TWENTY-SEVENTH SUNDAY IN ORDINARY TIME

First Reading: Habakkuk 1: 2-3; 2: 2-4

² Yahweh,[‡] how long will I cry, and you will not hear? I cry out to you "Violence!" and will you not save? ³ Why do you show me iniquity, and look at perversity? For destruction and violence are before me. There is strife, and contention rises up.
² Yahweh answered me, "Write the vision, and make it plain on tablets, that he who runs may read it. ³ For the vision is yet for the appointed time, and it hurries toward the end, and won't prove false. Though it takes time, wait for it, because it will surely come. It won't delay. ⁴ Behold, his soul is puffed up. It is not upright in him, but the righteous will live by his faith.

Responsorial Psalm: Psalms 95: 1-2, 6-7, 8-9

¹ Oh come, let's sing to Yahweh.
Let's shout aloud to the rock of our salvation!
² Let's come before his presence with thanksgiving.
Let's extol him with songs!
⁶ Oh come, let's worship and bow down.
Let's kneel before Yahweh, our Maker,
⁷ for he is our God.
We are the people of his pasture,

and the sheep in his care.
Today, oh that you would hear his voice!
8 Don't harden your heart, as at Meribah,
as in the day of Massah in the wilderness,
9 when your fathers tempted me,
tested me, and saw my work.

Second Reading: Second Timothy 1: 6-8, 13-14

6 For this cause, I remind you that you should stir up the gift of God which is in you through the laying on of my hands. 7 For God didn't give us a spirit of fear, but of power, love, and self-control. 8 Therefore don't be ashamed of the testimony of our Lord, nor of me his prisoner; but endure hardship for the Good News according to the power of God,
13 Hold the pattern of sound words which you have heard from me, in faith and love which is in Christ Jesus. 14 That good thing which was committed to you, guard through the Holy Spirit who dwells in us.

Gospel: Luke 17: 5-10

5 The apostles said to the Lord, "Increase our faith."
6 The Lord said, "If you had faith like a grain of mustard seed, you would tell this sycamore tree, 'Be uprooted and be planted in the sea,' and it would obey you. 7 But who is there among you, having a servant plowing or keeping sheep, that will say when he comes in from the field, 'Come immediately and sit down at the table'? 8 Wouldn't he rather tell him, 'Prepare my supper, clothe yourself properly, and serve me while I eat and drink. Afterward you shall eat and drink'? 9 Does he thank that servant because he did the things that were commanded? I think not. 10 Even so you also, when you have done all the things that are commanded you, say, 'We are unworthy servants. We have done our duty.' "

1. Invite the Holy Spirit into this reading, asking the Author of Scripture to speak to you through His Word
2. Read today's passage as many times as you need, take your time
3. Write down (below) what the Lord is saying to you today
4. Live with this Word in your heart through the day

_____

_____

Sunday, October 12, 2025
TWENTY-EIGHTH SUNDAY IN ORDINARY TIME

First Reading: Second Kings 5: 14-17

[14] Then went he down and dipped himself seven times in the Jordan, according to the saying of the man of God; and his flesh was restored like the flesh of a little child, and he was clean. [15] He returned to the man of God, he and all his company, and came, and stood before him; and he said, "See now, I know that there is no God in all the earth, but in Israel. Now therefore, please take a gift from your servant."
[16] But he said, "As Yahweh lives, before whom I stand, I will receive none."
He urged him to take it; but he refused. [17] Naaman said, "If not, then, please let two mules' load of earth be given to your servant; for your servant will from now on offer neither burnt offering nor sacrifice to other gods, but to Yahweh.

Responsorial Psalm: Psalms 98: 1, 2-3ab, 3c-4

[1] Sing to Yahweh a new song,
for he has done marvelous things!
His right hand and his holy arm have worked salvation for him.
[2] Yahweh has made known his salvation.
He has openly shown his righteousness in the sight of the nations.
[3] He has remembered his loving kindness and his faithfulness toward the house of Israel.
All the ends of the earth have seen the salvation of our God.
[4] Make a joyful noise to Yahweh, all the earth!
Burst out and sing for joy, yes, sing praises!

Second Reading: Second Timothy 2: 8-13

[8] Remember Jesus Christ, risen from the dead, of the offspring‡ of David, according to my Good News, [9] in which I suffer hardship to the point of chains as a criminal. But God's word isn't chained. [10] Therefore I endure all things for the chosen ones' sake, that they also may obtain the salvation which is in Christ Jesus with eternal glory. [11] This saying is trustworthy:
"For if we died with him,
we will also live with him.
[12] If we endure,
we will also reign with him.
If we deny him,
he also will deny us.

¹³ If we are faithless,
he remains faithful;
for he can't deny himself."

Gospel: Luke 17: 11-19

¹¹ As he was on his way to Jerusalem, he was passing along the borders of Samaria and Galilee. ¹² As he entered into a certain village, ten men who were lepers met him, who stood at a distance. ¹³ They lifted up their voices, saying, "Jesus, Master, have mercy on us!"
¹⁴ When he saw them, he said to them, "Go and show yourselves to the priests." As they went, they were cleansed. ¹⁵ One of them, when he saw that he was healed, turned back, glorifying God with a loud voice. ¹⁶ He fell on his face at Jesus' feet, giving him thanks; and he was a Samaritan.
¹⁷ Jesus answered, "Weren't the ten cleansed? But where are the nine? ¹⁸ Were there none found who returned to give glory to God, except this foreigner?" ¹⁹ Then he said to him, "Get up, and go your way. Your faith has healed you."

1. Invite the Holy Spirit into this reading, asking the Author of Scripture to speak to you through His Word
2. Read today's passage as many times as you need, take your time
3. Write down (below) what the Lord is saying to you today
4. Live with this Word in your heart through the day

_____

_____

Sunday, October 19, 2025
TWENTY-NINTH SUNDAY IN ORDINARY TIME

First Reading: Exodus 17: 8-13

⁸ Then Amalek came and fought with Israel in Rephidim. ⁹ Moses said to Joshua, "Choose men for us, and go out to fight with Amalek. Tomorrow I will stand on the top of the hill with God's rod in my hand." ¹⁰ So Joshua did as Moses had told him, and fought with Amalek; and Moses, Aaron, and Hur went up to the top of the hill. ¹¹ When Moses held up his hand, Israel prevailed. When he let down his hand, Amalek prevailed. ¹² But Moses' hands were heavy; so they took a stone, and put it under him, and he sat on it. Aaron and Hur held up his hands, the one on the one side, and the other on the other side. His hands

were steady until sunset. ¹³ Joshua defeated Amalek and his people with the edge of the sword.

Responsorial Psalm: Psalms 121: 1-2, 3-4, 5-6, 7-8

¹ I will lift up my eyes to the hills.
Where does my help come from?
² My help comes from Yahweh,
who made heaven and earth.
³ He will not allow your foot to be moved.
He who keeps you will not slumber.
⁴ Behold, he who keeps Israel
will neither slumber nor sleep.
⁵ Yahweh is your keeper.
Yahweh is your shade on your right hand.
⁶ The sun will not harm you by day,
nor the moon by night.
⁷ Yahweh will keep you from all evil.
He will keep your soul.
⁸ Yahweh will keep your going out and your coming in,
from this time forward, and forever more.

Second Reading: Second Timothy 3: 14 – 4: 2

¹⁴ But you remain in the things which you have learned and have been assured of, knowing from whom you have learned them. ¹⁵ From infancy, you have known the holy Scriptures which are able to make you wise for salvation through faith which is in Christ Jesus. ¹⁶ Every Scripture is God-breathed and‡ profitable for teaching, for reproof, for correction, and for instruction in righteousness, ¹⁷ that each person who belongs to God may be complete, thoroughly equipped for every good work.
¹ I command you therefore before God and the Lord Jesus Christ, who will judge the living and the dead at his appearing and his Kingdom: ² preach the word; be urgent in season and out of season; reprove, rebuke, and exhort with all patience and teaching.

Gospel: Luke 18: 1-8

¹ He also spoke a parable to them that they must always pray and not give up, ² saying, "There was a judge in a certain city who didn't fear God and didn't respect man. ³ A widow was in that city, and she often came to him, saying, 'Defend me from my adversary!' ⁴ He wouldn't for a while; but afterward he said to himself, 'Though I neither

fear God nor respect man, 5 yet because this widow bothers me, I will defend her, or else she will wear me out by her continual coming.' "

6 The Lord said, "Listen to what the unrighteous judge says. 7 Won't God avenge his chosen ones who are crying out to him day and night, and yet he exercises patience with them? 8 I tell you that he will avenge them quickly. Nevertheless, when the Son of Man comes, will he find faith on the earth?"

1. Invite the Holy Spirit into this reading, asking the Author of Scripture to speak to you through His Word
2. Read today's passage as many times as you need, take your time
3. Write down (below) what the Lord is saying to you today
4. Live with this Word in your heart through the day

Sunday, October 26, 2025
THIRTIETH SUNDAY IN ORDINARY TIME

First Reading: Sirach 35: 12-14, 16-18

12 Don't plan to bribe him with gifts, for he will not receive them.
Don't set your mind on an unrighteous sacrifice,
For the Lord is the judge,
and with him is no respect of persons.
13 He won't accept any person against a poor man.
He will listen to the prayer of him who is wronged.
14 He will in no way despise the supplication of the fatherless
or the widow, when she pours out her tale.
16 He who serves God according to his good pleasure will be accepted.
His supplication will reach to the clouds.
17 The prayer of the humble pierces the clouds.
until it comes near, he will not be comforted.
He won't depart until the Most High visits
and he judges righteously and executes judgment.
18 And the Lord will not be slack, neither will he be patient toward them,
until he has crushed the loins of the unmerciful.
He will repay vengeance to the heathen

until he has taken away the multitude of the arrogant
and broken in pieces the sceptres of the unrighteous,

Responsorial Psalm: Psalms 34: 2-3, 17-18, 19

2 My soul shall boast in Yahweh.
The humble shall hear of it and be glad.
3 Oh magnify Yahweh with me.
Let's exalt his name together.
17 The righteous cry, and Yahweh hears,
and delivers them out of all their troubles.
18 Yahweh is near to those who have a broken heart,
and saves those who have a crushed spirit.
19 Many are the afflictions of the righteous,
but Yahweh delivers him out of them all.

Second Reading: Second Timothy 4: 6-8, 16-18

6 For I am already being offered, and the time of my departure has come. 7 I have fought the good fight. I have finished the course. I have kept the faith. 8 From now on, the crown of righteousness is stored up for me, which the Lord, the righteous judge, will give to me on that day; and not to me only, but also to all those who have loved his appearing.
16 At my first defense, no one came to help me, but all left me. May it not be held against them. 17 But the Lord stood by me and strengthened me, that through me the message might be fully proclaimed, and that all the Gentiles might hear. So I was delivered out of the mouth of the lion. 18 And the Lord will deliver me from every evil work and will preserve me for his heavenly Kingdom. To him be the glory forever and ever. Amen.

Gospel: Luke 18: 9-14

9 He also spoke this parable to certain people who were convinced of their own righteousness, and who despised all others: 10 "Two men went up into the temple to pray; one was a Pharisee, and the other was a tax collector. 11 The Pharisee stood and prayed by himself like this: 'God, I thank you that I am not like the rest of men: extortionists, unrighteous, adulterers, or even like this tax collector. 12 I fast twice a week. I give tithes of all that I get.' 13 But the tax collector, standing far away, wouldn't even lift up his eyes to heaven, but beat his chest, saying, 'God, be merciful to me, a sinner!' 14 I tell you, this man went down to his house justified rather than the other; for everyone who exalts himself will be humbled, but he who humbles himself will be exalted."

1. Invite the Holy Spirit into this reading, asking the Author of Scripture to speak to you through His Word
2. Read today's passage as many times as you need, take your time
3. Write down (below) what the Lord is saying to you today
4. Live with this Word in your heart through the day

_____

_____

Sunday, November 2, 2025
THE COMMEMORATION OF ALL THE FAITHFUL DEPARTED (All Souls' Day)

First Reading: Wisdom 3: 1-9

¹ But the souls of the righteous are in the hand of God,
and no torment will touch them.
² In the eyes of the foolish they seemed to have died.
Their departure was considered a disaster,
³ and their travel away from us ruin,
but they are in peace.
⁴ For even if in the sight of men they are punished,
their hope is full of immortality.
⁵ Having borne a little chastening, they will receive great good;
because God tested them, and found them worthy of himself.
⁶ He tested them like gold in the furnace,
and he accepted them as a whole burnt offering.
⁷ In the time of their visitation they will shine.
They will run back and forth like sparks among stubble.
⁸ They will judge nations and have dominion over peoples.
The Lord will reign over them forever.
⁹ Those who trust him will understand truth.
The faithful will live with him in love,
because grace and mercy are with his chosen ones.

Responsorial Psalm: Psalms 23: 1-3a, 3b-4, 5, 6

¹ Yahweh is my shepherd;
I shall lack nothing.

2 He makes me lie down in green pastures.

He leads me beside still waters.

3 He restores my soul.

He guides me in the paths of righteousness for his name's sake.

4 Even though I walk through the valley of the shadow of death,

I will fear no evil, for you are with me.

Your rod and your staff,

they comfort me.

5 You prepare a table before me

in the presence of my enemies.

You anoint my head with oil.

My cup runs over.

6 Surely goodness and loving kindness shall follow me all the days of my life,

and I will dwell in Yahweh's house forever.

Second Reading: Romans 6: 3-9

3 Or don't you know that all of us who were baptized into Christ Jesus were baptized into his death? 4 We were buried therefore with him through baptism into death, that just as Christ was raised from the dead through the glory of the Father, so we also might walk in newness of life.

5 For if we have become united with him in the likeness of his death, we will also be part of his resurrection; 6 knowing this, that our old man was crucified with him, that the body of sin might be done away with, so that we would no longer be in bondage to sin. 7 For he who has died has been freed from sin. 8 But if we died with Christ, we believe that we will also live with him, 9 knowing that Christ, being raised from the dead, dies no more. Death no longer has dominion over him!

Gospel: John 6: 37-40

37 All those whom the Father gives me will come to me. He who comes to me I will in no way throw out. 38 For I have come down from heaven, not to do my own will, but the will of him who sent me. 39 This is the will of my Father who sent me, that of all he has given to me I should lose nothing, but should raise him up at the last day. 40 This is the will of the one who sent me, that everyone who sees the Son and believes in him should have eternal life; and I will raise him up at the last day."

1. Invite the Holy Spirit into this reading, asking the Author of Scripture to speak to you through His Word

2. Read today's passage as many times as you need, take your time

3. Write down (below) what the Lord is saying to you today
4. Live with this Word in your heart through the day

_____

_____

Sunday, November 9, 2025
THE DEDICATION OF THE LATERAN BASILICA

First Reading: Ezekiel 47: 1-2, 8-9, 12

[1] He brought me back to the door of the temple; and behold, waters flowed out from under the threshold of the temple eastward, for the front of the temple faced toward the east. The waters came down from underneath, from the right side of the temple, on the south of the altar. [2] Then he brought me out by the way of the gate northward, and led me around by the way outside to the outer gate, by the way of the gate that looks toward the east. Behold, waters ran out on the right side.

[8] Then he said to me, "These waters flow out toward the eastern region and will go down into the Arabah. Then they will go toward the sea and flow into the sea which will be made to flow out; and the waters will be healed. [9] It will happen that every living creature which swarms, in every place where the rivers come, will live. Then there will be a very great multitude of fish; for these waters have come there, and the waters of the sea will be healed, and everything will live wherever the river comes.

[12] By the river banks, on both sides, will grow every tree for food, whose leaf won't wither, neither will its fruit fail. It will produce new fruit every month, because its waters issue out of the sanctuary. Its fruit will be for food, and its leaf for healing."

Responsorial Psalm: Psalms 46: 2-3, 5-6, 8-9

[2] Therefore we won't be afraid, though the earth changes,
though the mountains are shaken into the heart of the seas;
[3] though its waters roar and are troubled,
though the mountains tremble with their swelling.
[5] God is within her. She shall not be moved.
God will help her at dawn.
[6] The nations raged. The kingdoms were moved.
He lifted his voice and the earth melted.
[8] Come, see Yahweh's works,

what desolations he has made in the earth.
⁹ He makes wars cease to the end of the earth.
He breaks the bow, and shatters the spear.
He burns the chariots in the fire.

Second Reading: First Corinthians 3: 9c-11, 16-17

⁹ᶜ You are God's farming, God's building.
¹⁰ According to the grace of God which was given to me, as a wise master builder I laid a foundation, and another builds on it. But let each man be careful how he builds on it. ¹¹ For no one can lay any other foundation than that which has been laid, which is Jesus Christ. ¹⁶ Don't you know that you are God's temple and that God's Spirit lives in you? ¹⁷ If anyone destroys God's temple, God will destroy him; for God's temple is holy, which you are.

Gospel: John 2: 13-22

¹³ The Passover of the Jews was at hand, and Jesus went up to Jerusalem. ¹⁴ He found in the temple those who sold oxen, sheep, and doves, and the changers of money sitting. ¹⁵ He made a whip of cords and drove all out of the temple, both the sheep and the oxen; and he poured out the changers' money and overthrew their tables. ¹⁶ To those who sold the doves, he said, "Take these things out of here! Don't make my Father's house a marketplace!" ¹⁷ His disciples remembered that it was written, "Zeal for your house will eat me up."*
¹⁸ The Jews therefore answered him, "What sign do you show us, seeing that you do these things?"
¹⁹ Jesus answered them, "Destroy this temple, and in three days I will raise it up."
²⁰ The Jews therefore said, "It took forty-six years to build this temple! Will you raise it up in three days?" ²¹ But he spoke of the temple of his body. ²² When therefore he was raised from the dead, his disciples remembered that he said this, and they believed the Scripture and the word which Jesus had said.

1. Invite the Holy Spirit into this reading, asking the Author of Scripture to speak to you through His Word
2. Read today's passage as many times as you need, take your time
3. Write down (below) what the Lord is saying to you today
4. Live with this Word in your heart through the day

_____

_____

First Reading: Malachi 4: 1-2a

[1] "For behold, the day comes, burning like a furnace, when all the proud and all who work wickedness will be stubble. The day that comes will burn them up," says Yahweh of Armies, "so that it will leave them neither root nor branch. [2] But to you who fear my name shall the sun of righteousness arise with healing in its wings.

Responsorial Psalm: Psalms 98: 5-6, 7-8, 9

[5] Sing praises to Yahweh with the harp,
with the harp and the voice of melody.
[6] With trumpets and sound of the ram's horn,
make a joyful noise before the King, Yahweh.
[7] Let the sea roar with its fullness;
the world, and those who dwell therein.
[8] Let the rivers clap their hands.
Let the mountains sing for joy together.
[9] Let them sing before Yahweh,
for he comes to judge the earth.
He will judge the world with righteousness,
and the peoples with equity.

Second Reading: Second Thessalonians 3: 7-12

[7] For you know how you ought to imitate us. For we didn't behave ourselves rebelliously among you, [8] neither did we eat bread from anyone's hand without paying for it, but in labor and travail worked night and day, that we might not burden any of you. [9] This was not because we don't have the right, but to make ourselves an example to you, that you should imitate us. [10] For even when we were with you, we commanded you this: "If anyone is not willing to work, don't let him eat." [11] For we hear of some who walk among you in rebellion, who don't work at all, but are busybodies. [12] Now those who are that way, we command and exhort in the Lord Jesus Christ, that they work with quietness and eat their own bread.

Gospel: Luke 21: 5-19

5 As some were talking about the temple and how it was decorated with beautiful stones and gifts, he said, 6 "As for these things which you see, the days will come in which there will not be left here one stone on another that will not be thrown down."

7 They asked him, "Teacher, so when will these things be? What is the sign that these things are about to happen?"

8 He said, "Watch out that you don't get led astray, for many will come in my name, saying, 'I am he‡,' and, 'The time is at hand.' Therefore don't follow them. 9 When you hear of wars and disturbances, don't be terrified, for these things must happen first, but the end won't come immediately."

10 Then he said to them, "Nation will rise against nation, and kingdom against kingdom. 11 There will be great earthquakes, famines, and plagues in various places. There will be terrors and great signs from heaven. 12 But before all these things, they will lay their hands on you and will persecute you, delivering you up to synagogues and prisons, bringing you before kings and governors for my name's sake. 13 It will turn out as a testimony for you. 14 Settle it therefore in your hearts not to meditate beforehand how to answer, 15 for I will give you a mouth and wisdom which all your adversaries will not be able to withstand or to contradict. 16 You will be handed over even by parents, brothers, relatives, and friends. They will cause some of you to be put to death. 17 You will be hated by all men for my name's sake. 18 And not a hair of your head will perish.

19 "By your endurance you will win your lives.

1. Invite the Holy Spirit into this reading, asking the Author of Scripture to speak to you through His Word
2. Read today's passage as many times as you need, take your time
3. Write down (below) what the Lord is saying to you today
4. Live with this Word in your heart through the day

_____

_____

Sunday, November 23, 2025
OUR LORD JESUS CHRIST, KING OF THE UNIVERSE

First Reading: Second Samuel 5: 1-3

1 Then all the tribes of Israel came to David at Hebron and spoke, saying, "Behold, we are your bone and your flesh. 2 In times past, when Saul was king over us, it was you who led Israel out and in. Yahweh said to you, 'You will be shepherd of my people Israel, and you

will be prince over Israel.' " [3] So all the elders of Israel came to the king to Hebron, and King David made a covenant with them in Hebron before Yahweh; and they anointed David king over Israel.

Responsorial Psalm: Psalms 122: 1-2, 3-4ab, 4cd-5

[1] I was glad when they said to me,
"Let's go to Yahweh's house!"
[2] Our feet are standing within your gates, Jerusalem!
[3] Jerusalem is built as a city that is compact together,
[4] where the tribes go up, even Yah's tribes,
according to an ordinance for Israel,
to give thanks to Yahweh's name.
[5] For there are set thrones for judgment,
the thrones of David's house.

Second Reading: Colossians 1: 12-20

[12] giving thanks to the Father, who made us fit to be partakers of the inheritance of the saints in light, [13] who delivered us out of the power of darkness, and translated us into the Kingdom of the Son of his love, [14] in whom we have our redemption,[±] the forgiveness of our sins.
[15] He is the image of the invisible God, the firstborn of all creation. [16] For by him all things were created in the heavens and on the earth, visible things and invisible things, whether thrones or dominions or principalities or powers. All things have been created through him and for him. [17] He is before all things, and in him all things are held together. [18] He is the head of the body, the assembly, who is the beginning, the firstborn from the dead, that in all things he might have the preeminence. [19] For all the fullness was pleased to dwell in him, [20] and through him to reconcile all things to himself by him, whether things on the earth or things in the heavens, having made peace through the blood of his cross.

Gospel: Luke 23: 35-43

[35] The people stood watching. The rulers with them also scoffed at him, saying, "He saved others. Let him save himself, if this is the Christ of God, his chosen one!"
[36] The soldiers also mocked him, coming to him and offering him vinegar, [37] and saying, "If you are the King of the Jews, save yourself!"
[38] An inscription was also written over him in letters of Greek, Latin, and Hebrew: "THIS IS THE KING OF THE JEWS."

³⁹ One of the criminals who was hanged insulted him, saying, "If you are the Christ, save yourself and us!"

⁴⁰ But the other answered, and rebuking him said, "Don't you even fear God, seeing you are under the same condemnation? ⁴¹ And we indeed justly, for we receive the due reward for our deeds, but this man has done nothing wrong." ⁴² He said to Jesus, "Lord, remember me when you come into your Kingdom."

⁴³ Jesus said to him, "Assuredly I tell you, today you will be with me in Paradise."

1. Invite the Holy Spirit into this reading, asking the Author of Scripture to speak to you through His Word
2. Read today's passage as many times as you need, take your time
3. Write down (below) what the Lord is saying to you today
4. Live with this Word in your heart through the day

Sunday, November 30, 2025
FIRST SUNDAY OF ADVENT

First Reading: Isaiah 2: 1-5

¹ This is what Isaiah the son of Amoz saw concerning Judah and Jerusalem.
² It shall happen in the latter days, that the mountain of Yahweh's house shall be established on the top of the mountains,
and shall be raised above the hills;
and all nations shall flow to it.
³ Many peoples shall go and say,
"Come, let's go up to the mountain of Yahweh,
to the house of the God of Jacob;
and he will teach us of his ways,
and we will walk in his paths."
For the law shall go out of Zion,
and Yahweh's word from Jerusalem.
⁴ He will judge between the nations,
and will decide concerning many peoples.
They shall beat their swords into plowshares,
and their spears into pruning hooks.

Nation shall not lift up sword against nation,
neither shall they learn war any more.
⁵ House of Jacob, come, and let's walk in the light of Yahweh.

Responsorial Psalm: Psalms 122: 1-2, 3-4ab, 4cd-5, 6-7, 8-9

¹ I was glad when they said to me,
"Let's go to Yahweh's house!"
² Our feet are standing within your gates, Jerusalem!
³ Jerusalem is built as a city that is compact together,
⁴ where the tribes go up, even Yah's tribes,
according to an ordinance for Israel,
to give thanks to Yahweh's name.
⁵ For there are set thrones for judgment,
the thrones of David's house.
⁶ Pray for the peace of Jerusalem.
Those who love you will prosper.
⁷ Peace be within your walls,
and prosperity within your palaces.
⁸ For my brothers' and companions' sakes,
I will now say, "Peace be within you."
⁹ For the sake of the house of Yahweh our God,
I will seek your good.

Second Reading: Romans 13: 11-14

¹¹ Do this, knowing the time, that it is already time for you to awaken out of sleep, for salvation is now nearer to us than when we first believed. ¹² The night is far gone, and the day is near. Let's therefore throw off the deeds of darkness, and let's put on the armor of light. ¹³ Let's walk properly, as in the day; not in reveling and drunkenness, not in sexual promiscuity and lustful acts, and not in strife and jealousy. ¹⁴ But put on the Lord Jesus Christ, and make no provision for the flesh, for its lusts.

Gospel: Matthew 24: 37-44

³⁷ As the days of Noah were, so will the coming of the Son of Man be. ³⁸ For as in those days which were before the flood they were eating and drinking, marrying and giving in marriage, until the day that Noah entered into the ship, ³⁹ and they didn't know until the flood came and took them all away, so will the coming of the Son of Man be. ⁴⁰ Then two men will be in the field: one will be taken and one will be left. ⁴¹ Two women will be

grinding at the mill: one will be taken and one will be left. 42 Watch therefore, for you don't know in what hour your Lord comes. 43 But know this, that if the master of the house had known in what watch of the night the thief was coming, he would have watched, and would not have allowed his house to be broken into. 44 Therefore also be ready, for in an hour that you don't expect, the Son of Man will come.

1. Invite the Holy Spirit into this reading, asking the Author of Scripture to speak to you through His Word
2. Read today's passage as many times as you need, take your time
3. Write down (below) what the Lord is saying to you today
4. Live with this Word in your heart through the day

Sunday, December 7, 2025
SECOND SUNDAY OF ADVENT

First Reading: Isaiah 11: 1-10

1 A shoot will come out of the stock of Jesse,
and a branch out of his roots will bear fruit.
2 Yahweh's Spirit will rest on him:
the spirit of wisdom and understanding,
the spirit of counsel and might,
the spirit of knowledge and of the fear of Yahweh.
3 His delight will be in the fear of Yahweh.
He will not judge by the sight of his eyes,
neither decide by the hearing of his ears;
4 but he will judge the poor with righteousness,
and decide with equity for the humble of the earth.
He will strike the earth with the rod of his mouth;
and with the breath of his lips he will kill the wicked.
5 Righteousness will be the belt around his waist,
and faithfulness the belt around his waist.
6 The wolf will live with the lamb,
and the leopard will lie down with the young goat,
the calf, the young lion, and the fattened calf together;

and a little child will lead them.

7 The cow and the bear will graze.

Their young ones will lie down together.

The lion will eat straw like the ox.

8 The nursing child will play near a cobra's hole,

and the weaned child will put his hand on the viper's den.

9 They will not hurt nor destroy in all my holy mountain;

for the earth will be full of the knowledge of Yahweh,

as the waters cover the sea.

10 It will happen in that day that the nations will seek the root of Jesse, who stands as a banner of the peoples; and his resting place will be glorious.

Responsorial Psalm: Psalms 72: 1-2, 7-8, 12-13, 17

1 God, give the king your justice;

your righteousness to the royal son.

2 He will judge your people with righteousness,

and your poor with justice.

7 In his days, the righteous shall flourish,

and abundance of peace, until the moon is no more.

8 He shall have dominion also from sea to sea,

from the River to the ends of the earth.

12 For he will deliver the needy when he cries;

the poor, who has no helper.

13 He will have pity on the poor and needy.

He will save the souls of the needy.

17 His name endures forever.

His name continues as long as the sun.

Men shall be blessed by him.

All nations will call him blessed.

Second Reading: Romans 15: 4-9

4 For whatever things were written before were written for our learning, that through perseverance and through encouragement of the Scriptures we might have hope. 5 Now the God of perseverance and of encouragement grant you to be of the same mind with one another according to Christ Jesus, 6 that with one accord you may with one mouth glorify the God and Father of our Lord Jesus Christ.

7 Therefore accept one another, even as Christ also accepted you,⁺ to the glory of God. 8 Now I say that Christ has been made a servant of the circumcision for the truth of God, that he

might confirm the promises given to the fathers, ⁹ and that the Gentiles might glorify God for his mercy. As it is written,
"Therefore I will give praise to you among the Gentiles
and sing to your name."

Gospel: Matthew 3: 1-12

¹ In those days, John the Baptizer came, preaching in the wilderness of Judea, saying, ² "Repent, for the Kingdom of Heaven is at hand!" ³ For this is he who was spoken of by Isaiah the prophet, saying,
"The voice of one crying in the wilderness,
make the way of the Lord ready!
Make his paths straight!"*
⁴ Now John himself wore clothing made of camel's hair with a leather belt around his waist. His food was locusts and wild honey. ⁵ Then people from Jerusalem, all of Judea, and all the region around the Jordan went out to him. ⁶ They were baptized by him in the Jordan, confessing their sins.
⁷ But when he saw many of the Pharisees and Sadducees coming for his baptism, he said to them, "You offspring of vipers, who warned you to flee from the wrath to come? ⁸ Therefore produce fruit worthy of repentance! ⁹ Don't think to yourselves, 'We have Abraham for our father,' for I tell you that God is able to raise up children to Abraham from these stones. ¹⁰ Even now the ax lies at the root of the trees. Therefore every tree that doesn't produce good fruit is cut down, and cast into the fire.
¹¹ "I indeed baptize you in water for repentance, but he who comes after me is mightier than I, whose sandals I am not worthy to carry. He will baptize you in the Holy Spirit.‡ ¹² His winnowing fork is in his hand, and he will thoroughly cleanse his threshing floor. He will gather his wheat into the barn, but the chaff he will burn up with unquenchable fire."

1. Invite the Holy Spirit into this reading, asking the Author of Scripture to speak to you through His Word
2. Read today's passage as many times as you need, take your time
3. Write down (below) what the Lord is saying to you today
4. Live with this Word in your heart through the day

_____

_____

First Reading: Isaiah 35: 1-6a, 10

[1] The wilderness and the dry land will be glad.
The desert will rejoice and blossom like a rose.
[2] It will blossom abundantly,
and rejoice even with joy and singing.
Lebanon's glory will be given to it,
the excellence of Carmel and Sharon.
They will see Yahweh's glory,
the excellence of our God.
[3] Strengthen the weak hands,
and make the feeble knees firm.
[4] Tell those who have a fearful heart, "Be strong!
Don't be afraid!
Behold, your God will come with vengeance, God's retribution.
He will come and save you.
[5] Then the eyes of the blind will be opened,
and the ears of the deaf will be unstopped.
[6] Then the lame man will leap like a deer,
and the tongue of the mute will sing;
for waters will break out in the wilderness,
and streams in the desert.
[10] Then Yahweh's ransomed ones will return,
and come with singing to Zion;
and everlasting joy will be on their heads.
They will obtain gladness and joy,
and sorrow and sighing will flee away."

Responsorial Psalm: Psalms 146: 6-7, 8-9a, 9bc-10

[6] who made heaven and earth,
the sea, and all that is in them;
who keeps truth forever;
[7] who executes justice for the oppressed;
who gives food to the hungry.
Yahweh frees the prisoners.
[8] Yahweh opens the eyes of the blind.

Yahweh raises up those who are bowed down.
Yahweh loves the righteous.
9 Yahweh preserves the foreigners.
He upholds the fatherless and widow,
but he turns the way of the wicked upside down.
10 Yahweh will reign forever;
your God, O Zion, to all generations.
Praise Yah!

Second Reading: James 5: 7-10

7 Be patient therefore, brothers, until the coming of the Lord. Behold, the farmer waits for the precious fruit of the earth, being patient over it, until it receives the early and late rain. 8 You also be patient. Establish your hearts, for the coming of the Lord is at hand.
9 Don't grumble, brothers, against one another, so that you won't be judged. Behold, the judge stands at the door. 10 Take, brothers, for an example of suffering and of perseverance, the prophets who spoke in the name of the Lord.

Gospel: Matthew 11: 2-11

2 Now when John heard in the prison the works of Christ, he sent two of his disciples 3 and said to him, "Are you he who comes, or should we look for another?"
4 Jesus answered them, "Go and tell John the things which you hear and see: 5 the blind receive their sight, the lame walk, the lepers are cleansed, the deaf hear,* the dead are raised up, and the poor have good news preached to them.* 6 Blessed is he who finds no occasion for stumbling in me."
7 As these went their way, Jesus began to say to the multitudes concerning John, "What did you go out into the wilderness to see? A reed shaken by the wind? 8 But what did you go out to see? A man in soft clothing? Behold, those who wear soft clothing are in kings' houses. 9 But why did you go out? To see a prophet? Yes, I tell you, and much more than a prophet. 10 For this is he, of whom it is written, 'Behold, I send my messenger before your face, who will prepare your way before you.'* 11 Most certainly I tell you, among those who are born of women there has not arisen anyone greater than John the Baptizer; yet he who is least in the Kingdom of Heaven is greater than he.

1. Invite the Holy Spirit into this reading, asking the Author of Scripture to speak to you through His Word
2. Read today's passage as many times as you need, take your time
3. Write down (below) what the Lord is saying to you today
4. Live with this Word in your heart through the day

Sunday, December 21, 2025
FOURTH SUNDAY OF ADVENT

First Reading: Isaiah 7: 10-14

10 Yahweh spoke again to Ahaz, saying, 11 "Ask a sign of Yahweh your God; ask it either in the depth, or in the height above."
12 But Ahaz said, "I won't ask. I won't tempt Yahweh."
13 He said, "Listen now, house of David. Is it not enough for you to try the patience of men, that you will try the patience of my God also? 14 Therefore the Lord himself will give you a sign. Behold, the virgin will conceive, and bear a son, and shall call his name Immanuel.

Responsorial Psalm: Psalms 24: 1-2, 3-4, 5-6

1 The earth is Yahweh's, with its fullness;
the world, and those who dwell in it.
2 For he has founded it on the seas,
and established it on the floods.
3 Who may ascend to Yahweh's hill?
Who may stand in his holy place?
4 He who has clean hands and a pure heart;
who has not lifted up his soul to falsehood,
and has not sworn deceitfully.
5 He shall receive a blessing from Yahweh,
righteousness from the God of his salvation.
6 This is the generation of those who seek Him,
who seek your face—even Jacob.

Second Reading: Romans 1: 1-7

1 Paul, a servant of Jesus Christ,‡ called to be an apostle, set apart for the Good News of God, 2 which he promised before through his prophets in the holy Scriptures, 3 concerning his Son, who was born of the offspring‡ of David according to the flesh, 4 who was declared to be the Son of God with power according to the Spirit of holiness, by the resurrection

from the dead, Jesus Christ our Lord, ⁵ through whom we received grace and apostleship for obedience of faith among all the nations for his name's sake; ⁶ among whom you are also called to belong to Jesus Christ; ⁷ to all who are in Rome, beloved of God, called to be saints: Grace to you and peace from God our Father and the Lord Jesus Christ.

Gospel: Matthew 1: 18-24

¹⁸ Now the birth of Jesus Christ was like this: After his mother, Mary, was engaged to Joseph, before they came together, she was found pregnant by the Holy Spirit. ¹⁹ Joseph, her husband, being a righteous man, and not willing to make her a public example, intended to put her away secretly. ²⁰ But when he thought about these things, behold,‡ an angel of the Lord appeared to him in a dream, saying, "Joseph, son of David, don't be afraid to take to yourself Mary as your wife, for that which is conceived in her is of the Holy Spirit. ²¹ She shall give birth to a son. You shall name him Jesus,‡ for it is he who shall save his people from their sins."
²² Now all this has happened that it might be fulfilled which was spoken by the Lord through the prophet, saying,
²³ "Behold, the virgin shall be with child,
and shall give birth to a son.
They shall call his name Immanuel,"
which is, being interpreted, "God with us."*
²⁴ Joseph arose from his sleep, and did as the angel of the Lord commanded him, and took his wife to himself;

1. Invite the Holy Spirit into this reading, asking the Author of Scripture to speak to you through His Word
2. Read today's passage as many times as you need, take your time
3. Write down (below) what the Lord is saying to you today
4. Live with this Word in your heart through the day

_____

_____

Wednesday, December 24, 2025

First Reading: Second Samuel 7: 1-5, 8b-12, 14a, 16

¹ When the king lived in his house, and Yahweh had given him rest from all his enemies all around, ² the king said to Nathan the prophet, "See now, I dwell in a house of cedar, but God's ark dwells within curtains."

³ Nathan said to the king, "Go, do all that is in your heart, for Yahweh is with you."

⁴ That same night, Yahweh's word came to Nathan, saying, ⁵ "Go and tell my servant David, 'Yahweh says, "Should you build me a house for me to dwell in?

⁸ Now therefore tell my servant David this: 'Yahweh of Armies says, "I took you from the sheep pen, from following the sheep, to be prince over my people, over Israel. ⁹ I have been with you wherever you went, and have cut off all your enemies from before you. I will make you a great name, like the name of the great ones who are in the earth. ¹⁰ I will appoint a place for my people Israel, and will plant them, that they may dwell in their own place and be moved no more. The children of wickedness will not afflict them any more, as at the first, ¹¹ and as from the day that I commanded judges to be over my people Israel. I will cause you to rest from all your enemies. Moreover Yahweh tells you that Yahweh will make you a house. ¹² When your days are fulfilled and you sleep with your fathers, I will set up your offspring after you, who will proceed out of your body, and I will establish his kingdom.

¹⁴ I will be his father, and he will be my son. If he commits iniquity, I will chasten him with the rod of men and with the stripes of the children of men;

¹⁶ Your house and your kingdom will be made sure forever before you. Your throne will be established forever." ' "

Responsorial Psalm: Psalms 89: 2-3, 4-5, 27 and 29

² I indeed declare, "Love stands firm forever.
You established the heavens.
Your faithfulness is in them."
³ "I have made a covenant with my chosen one,
I have sworn to David, my servant,
⁴ 'I will establish your offspring forever,
and build up your throne to all generations.' "
Selah.
⁵ The heavens will praise your wonders, Yahweh,
your faithfulness also in the assembly of the holy ones.
²⁷ I will also appoint him my firstborn,
the highest of the kings of the earth.
²⁹ I will also make his offspring endure forever,
and his throne as the days of heaven.

Gospel: Luke 1: 67-79

⁶⁷ His father Zacharias was filled with the Holy Spirit, and prophesied, saying,
⁶⁸ "Blessed be the Lord, the God of Israel,
for he has visited and redeemed his people;
⁶⁹ and has raised up a horn of salvation for us in the house of his servant David
⁷⁰ (as he spoke by the mouth of his holy prophets who have been from of old),
⁷¹ salvation from our enemies and from the hand of all who hate us;
⁷² to show mercy toward our fathers,
to remember his holy covenant,
⁷³ the oath which he swore to Abraham our father,
⁷⁴ to grant to us that we, being delivered out of the hand of our enemies,
should serve him without fear,
⁷⁵ in holiness and righteousness before him all the days of our life.
⁷⁶ And you, child, will be called a prophet of the Most High;
for you will go before the face of the Lord to prepare his ways,
⁷⁷ to give knowledge of salvation to his people by the remission of their sins,
⁷⁸ because of the tender mercy of our God,
by which the dawn from on high will visit us,
⁷⁹ to shine on those who sit in darkness and the shadow of death;
to guide our feet into the way of peace."

1. Invite the Holy Spirit into this reading, asking the Author of Scripture to speak to you through His Word
2. Read today's passage as many times as you need, take your time
3. Write down (below) what the Lord is saying to you today
4. Live with this Word in your heart through the day

_____

_____

Thursday, December 25, 2025
THE NATIVITY OF THE LORD (Christmas)

First Reading: Isaiah 52: 7-10

⁷ How beautiful on the mountains are the feet of him who brings good news,
who publishes peace,
who brings good news,

who proclaims salvation,

who says to Zion, "Your God reigns!"

[8] Your watchmen lift up their voice.

Together they sing;

for they shall see eye to eye when Yahweh returns to Zion.

[9] Break out into joy!

Sing together, you waste places of Jerusalem;

for Yahweh has comforted his people.

He has redeemed Jerusalem.

[10] Yahweh has made his holy arm bare in the eyes of all the nations.

All the ends of the earth have seen the salvation of our God.

Responsorial Psalm: Psalms 98: 1, 2-3, 3-4, 5-6

[1] Sing to Yahweh a new song,

for he has done marvelous things!

His right hand and his holy arm have worked salvation for him.

[2] Yahweh has made known his salvation.

He has openly shown his righteousness in the sight of the nations.

[3] He has remembered his loving kindness and his faithfulness toward the house of Israel.

All the ends of the earth have seen the salvation of our God.

[4] Make a joyful noise to Yahweh, all the earth!

Burst out and sing for joy, yes, sing praises!

[5] Sing praises to Yahweh with the harp,

with the harp and the voice of melody.

[6] With trumpets and sound of the ram's horn,

make a joyful noise before the King, Yahweh.

Second Reading: Hebrews 1: 1-6

[1] God, having in the past spoken to the fathers through the prophets at many times and in various ways, [2] has at the end of these days spoken to us by his Son, whom he appointed heir of all things, through whom also he made the worlds. [3] His Son is the radiance of his glory, the very image of his substance, and upholding all things by the word of his power, who, when he had by himself purified us of our sins, sat down on the right hand of the Majesty on high, [4] having become as much better than the angels as the more excellent name he has inherited is better than theirs. [5] For to which of the angels did he say at any time,

"You are my Son.

Today I have become your father?"[*]

and again,

"I will be to him a Father,

and he will be to me a Son?"[*]

6 When he again brings in the firstborn into the world he says, "Let all the angels of God worship him."

Gospel: John 1: 1-18

1 In the beginning was the Word, and the Word was with God, and the Word was God. 2 The same was in the beginning with God. 3 All things were made through him. Without him, nothing was made that has been made. 4 In him was life, and the life was the light of men. 5 The light shines in the darkness, and the darkness hasn't overcome[†] it.

6 There came a man sent from God, whose name was John. 7 The same came as a witness, that he might testify about the light, that all might believe through him. 8 He was not the light, but was sent that he might testify about the light. 9 The true light that enlightens everyone was coming into the world.

10 He was in the world, and the world was made through him, and the world didn't recognize him. 11 He came to his own, and those who were his own didn't receive him. 12 But as many as received him, to them he gave the right to become God's children, to those who believe in his name: 13 who were born, not of blood, nor of the will of the flesh, nor of the will of man, but of God.

14 The Word became flesh and lived among us. We saw his glory, such glory as of the only born[‡] Son of the Father, full of grace and truth. 15 John testified about him. He cried out, saying, "This was he of whom I said, 'He who comes after me has surpassed me, for he was before me.' " 16 From his fullness we all received grace upon grace. 17 For the law was given through Moses. Grace and truth were realized through Jesus Christ.[§] 18 No one has seen God at any time. The only born[‡] Son,[‡] who is in the bosom of the Father, has declared him.

1. Invite the Holy Spirit into this reading, asking the Author of Scripture to speak to you through His Word

2. Read today's passage as many times as you need, take your time

3. Write down (below) what the Lord is saying to you today

4. Live with this Word in your heart through the day

_____

_____

Friday, December 26, 2025
Saint Stephen, the First Martyr

First Reading: Acts 6: 8-10; 7: 54-59

8 Stephen, full of faith and power, performed great wonders and signs among the people. 9 But some of those who were of the synagogue called "The Libertines", and of the Cyrenians, of the Alexandrians, and of those of Cilicia and Asia arose, disputing with Stephen. 10 They weren't able to withstand the wisdom and the Spirit by which he spoke. 54 Now when they heard these things, they were cut to the heart, and they gnashed at him with their teeth. 55 But he, being full of the Holy Spirit, looked up steadfastly into heaven and saw the glory of God, and Jesus standing on the right hand of God, 56 and said, "Behold, I see the heavens opened and the Son of Man standing at the right hand of God!" 57 But they cried out with a loud voice and stopped their ears, then rushed at him with one accord. 58 They threw him out of the city and stoned him. The witnesses placed their garments at the feet of a young man named Saul. 59 They stoned Stephen as he called out, saying, "Lord Jesus, receive my spirit!"

Responsorial Psalm: Psalms 31: 3cd-4, 6 and 8ab, 16bc and 17

3 For you are my rock and my fortress,
therefore for your name's sake lead me and guide me.
4 Pluck me out of the net that they have laid secretly for me,
for you are my stronghold.
6 I hate those who regard lying vanities,
but I trust in Yahweh.
8 You have not shut me up into the hand of the enemy.
You have set my feet in a large place.
16 Make your face to shine on your servant.
Save me in your loving kindness.
17 Let me not be disappointed, Yahweh, for I have called on you.
Let the wicked be disappointed.
Let them be silent in Sheol.

Gospel: Matthew 10: 17-22

17 But beware of men, for they will deliver you up to councils, and in their synagogues they will scourge you. 18 Yes, and you will be brought before governors and kings for my sake, for a testimony to them and to the nations. 19 But when they deliver you up, don't be

anxious how or what you will say, for it will be given you in that hour what you will say. ²⁰ For it is not you who speak, but the Spirit of your Father who speaks in you. ²¹ "Brother will deliver up brother to death, and the father his child. Children will rise up against parents and cause them to be put to death. ²² You will be hated by all men for my name's sake, but he who endures to the end will be saved.

1. Invite the Holy Spirit into this reading, asking the Author of Scripture to speak to you through His Word
2. Read today's passage as many times as you need, take your time
3. Write down (below) what the Lord is saying to you today
4. Live with this Word in your heart through the day

_____

_____

Sunday, December 28, 2025
THE HOLY FAMILY OF JESUS, MARY AND JOSEPH

First Reading: Sirach 3: 2-6, 12-14

² For the Lord honors the father over the children,
and has confirmed the judgment of the mother over her sons.
³ He who honors his father will make atonement for sins.
⁴ He who gives glory to his mother is as one who lays up treasure.
⁵ Whoever honors his father will have joy in his own children.
He will be heard in the day of his prayer.
⁶ He who gives glory to his father will have length of days.
He who listens to the Lord will bring rest to his mother,
¹² My son, help your father in his old age,
and don't grieve him as long as he lives.
¹³ If he fails in understanding, have patience with him.
Don't dishonor him in your full strength.
¹⁴ For the kindness to your father will not be forgotten.
Instead of sins it will be added to build you up.

Responsorial Psalm: Psalms 128: 1-2, 3, 4-5

¹ Blessed is everyone who fears Yahweh,

who walks in his ways.

2 For you will eat the labor of your hands.
You will be happy, and it will be well with you.
3 Your wife will be as a fruitful vine in the innermost parts of your house,
your children like olive shoots around your table.
4 Behold, this is how the man who fears Yahweh is blessed.
5 May Yahweh bless you out of Zion,
and may you see the good of Jerusalem all the days of your life.

Second Reading: Colossians 3: 12-17

12 Put on therefore, as God's chosen ones, holy and beloved, a heart of compassion, kindness, lowliness, humility, and perseverance; 13 bearing with one another, and forgiving each other, if any man has a complaint against any; even as Christ forgave you, so you also do.
14 Above all these things, walk in love, which is the bond of perfection. 15 And let the peace of God rule in your hearts, to which also you were called in one body, and be thankful. 16 Let the word of Christ dwell in you richly; in all wisdom teaching and admonishing one another with psalms, hymns, and spiritual songs, singing with grace in your heart to the Lord.
17 Whatever you do, in word or in deed, do all in the name of the Lord Jesus, giving thanks to God the Father through him.

Gospel: Matthew 2: 13-15, 19-23

13 Now when they had departed, behold, an angel of the Lord appeared to Joseph in a dream, saying, "Arise and take the young child and his mother, and flee into Egypt, and stay there until I tell you, for Herod will seek the young child to destroy him."
14 He arose and took the young child and his mother by night and departed into Egypt, 15 and was there until the death of Herod, that it might be fulfilled which was spoken by the Lord through the prophet, saying, "Out of Egypt I called my son."*
19 But when Herod was dead, behold, an angel of the Lord appeared in a dream to Joseph in Egypt, saying, 20 "Arise and take the young child and his mother, and go into the land of Israel, for those who sought the young child's life are dead."
21 He arose and took the young child and his mother, and came into the land of Israel. 22 But when he heard that Archelaus was reigning over Judea in the place of his father, Herod, he was afraid to go there. Being warned in a dream, he withdrew into the region of Galilee, 23 and came and lived in a city called Nazareth; that it might be fulfilled which was spoken through the prophets that he will be called a Nazarene.

1. Invite the Holy Spirit into this reading, asking the Author of Scripture to speak to you through His Word
2. Read today's passage as many times as you need, take your time
3. Write down (below) what the Lord is saying to you today
4. Live with this Word in your heart through the day

_____

_____